8-CIRCUIT ASCENSION WORKBOOK

Some Other Titles from Falcon Press

Douglas S. Wingate & Rachel Turetzky, Ph.D.
8-Circuit Ascension: A Guide to Metaprogramming the Multidimensional Self

Antero Alli
The Eight-Circuit Brain: Navigational Strategies for the Energetic Body
Eight-Circuits of Consciousness (video)
Angel Tech: A Modern Shaman's Guide to Reality Selection

Christopher S. Hyatt, Ph.D.
Undoing Yourself with Energized Meditation and Other Devices
Secrets of Western Tantra: The Sexuality of the Middle Path

Steven Heller
Monsters & Magical Sticks: There's No Such Thing As Hypnosis?

Peter J. Carroll
The Chaos Magick Audios
PsyberMagick

Phil Hine
Condensed Chaos: An Introduction to Chaos Magic
Prime Chaos: Adventures in Chaos Magic
Queerying Occultures

Joseph Lisiewski, Ph.D.
A Kabbalistic Handbook for the Practicing Magician
Ceremonial Magic & the Power of Evocation

Israel Regardie
The Complete Golden Dawn System of Magic
The Golden Dawn Audios

Denny Sargent
Naga Magick: The Wisdom of the Serpent Lords
Tantra for All: The Path of Nath Tantrika

Gregory Peters
Yogini Magic: Sorcery, Enchantment & Witchcraft of the Divine Feminine
New Aeon Tantra: Secrets of Typhonian Magick & Western Tantra

For up-to-the-minute information on prices and availability, please visit our website at originalfalcon.com

8-Circuit Ascension Workbook

Tools to Change Your Brain & Increase Intelligence

by
Douglas S. Wingate &
Rachel Turetzky, Ph.D.

The *Original* Falcon Press
Tempe, Arizona, U.S.A.

International Standard Book Number: 978-1-61869-643-4
ISBN: 978-1-61869-644-1 (mobi)
ISBN: 978-1-61869-645-8 (ePub)

First Print Edition 2026
First eBook Edition 2026

Logo Design/Cover Image by Rachel Turetzky and Rob Randolph
Cover Design by Douglas Wingate

The paper used in this publication meets the minimum requirements of the American National Standard for Permanence of Paper for Printed Library Materials Z39.48-1984

Address all inquiries to:
The Original Falcon Press
1753 East Broadway Road #101-277
Tempe, AZ 85282 U.S.A.
(or)
PO Box 3540
Silver Springs NV 89429 U.S.A.
website: originalfalcon.com
email: info@originalfalcon.com

Dedication

To all the brave psychonauts and metaprogrammers who undertake the Great Work of self-transformation:

Thank you for following the call and doing the Work—that the world may become a better place with each person who chooses to heal and to evolve with intention.

CONTENTS

Preface

This Workbook is based on—and is intended to supplement and be used alongside—our primary text, *8-Circuit Ascension: A Guide to Metaprogramming the Multidimensional Self* (2025; referred to henceforth as "the Guide"). While the Guide provides dense academic discussion, references, and citations, this Workbook focuses on practical elements and direct application. It is aimed at healing, better navigating, and improving the overall human experience by making the understanding of these states and parts of yourself approachable in both self-work and clinical therapy.

Who Is This Workbook For?

This Workbook is designed to serve several distinct audiences:

- **Mental Health and Clinical Professionals:** For practitioners, this serves as a resource of practical tools and exercises for themselves and their clients to explore experiences related to each of the Eight Circuits of Consciousness. It offers a sound framework for those working within the resurging cultural momentum of psychedelic-assisted psychotherapy.
- **Non-Professionals and Seekers:** For those who have not read the Guide and want a less academic, more accessible presentation of the model, this Workbook acts as a standalone "playbook for transformation." It is crafted for the seeker, healer, or adventurer who desires a map to expand their inner world.
- **Active Explorers:** Regardless of professional status, this book is for anyone who wants "things to do." If you are looking for a clear

structure to navigate and expand your consciousness through Reflections and Action Steps, this Workbook provides that practical path.

How Is This Book Organized?

The Workbook is organized into a logical progression:

- **Foundational Material** (Chapter 1): Provides the necessary terminology, history, and broad concepts (such as "reality tunnels" and "imprinting") to ground the rest of your work.
- **The Circuit Chapters** (Chapters 2–11): Each chapter is dedicated to a specific circuit (0 through 8) or a transitional state like "Chapel Perilous." Each follows a consistent three-part structure:
  - **Chapter Summary:** A brief overview of the extensive theory explored in the Guide.
  - **Reflections:** Targeted prompts to help you identify your personal imprints and belief structures.
  - **Action Steps:** Practical exercises, guided activities, and meditations designed to deepen your personal experience of that circuit.
- **Reference Tools:** A Glossary of Terms is included at the back to help you master the unique vocabulary of metaprogramming.

How Should the Book Be Used?

This book is intended for active participation. While it can be read straight through to understand the development of the circuits, it can also be used as a targeted manual to address specific circuit imbalances or "treadmilling" (becoming rigidly stuck in one part of yourself).

You may use it as a private journal for self-transformation; or if recommended by a practitioner, as a structured component of your therapeutic journey. We recommend recording your responses in the "Reflection" sections, and committing to the "Action Steps" for at least a week to allow your nervous system to integrate the new signals.

What Can You Expect to Get Out Of It?

By engaging with this material, you can expect to:

- **Gain a "Map" of Consciousness:** understand the filters (or "reality tunnels") through which you perceive the world.
- **Facilitate Metaprogramming:** Learn to consciously "re-imprint" or alter detrimental belief systems and rigid thought patterns that may have been hard-wired into your nervous system since childhood.
- **Increase Intelligence:** Use the "neuron model of intelligence" to better absorb, integrate, and transmit information, effectively "changing your brain."
- **Achieve Integration:** Most importantly, you will learn to bring the expansive wisdom gained through these experiences into your life to heal trauma and improve your daily interactions.

This workbook is your playbook for transformation. It is designed to help you navigate your own "reality tunnel," and reclaim the power to rewrite your own story. Whether you are a clinical professional or a brave psychonaut, we thank you for following the call to do the Work, knowing that the world becomes a better place with each person who chooses to heal and to evolve with intention. May this journey allow you to live fully awake and embodied, in harmony with the multidimensional spectrum of your own consciousness.

Chapter 1

History & Applications of The 8-Circuit Model

Chapter Summary

The 8-Circuit Model of Consciousness can be a useful tool to explore yourself, and to make meaning of previous and profound life experiences, for psychotherapeutic support, or integration of psychedelic and non-ordinary states of consciousness, all of which may have a strong influence on how we navigate the world. As we present it, the model is built from the works of Dr. Timothy Leary in *Exo-Psychology* (1977), *The Game of Life* (1978), and *Info-Psychology* (1987); various works by Robert Anton Wilson, most prominently *Prometheus Rising* (1983); those by Antero Alli—*Angel Tech* (1987) and *The Eight Circuit Brain* (2009); and our own, *8-Circuit Ascension: A Guide to Metaprogramming the Multidimensional Self* (2025). There are other contemporary authors who have approached this model as well; you can find them in the Bibliography chapter of the Guide.

The model exists as a meta-model, which means it offers a framework into which other models from psychology and spirituality can fit. It accounts for and offers ways of working with developmental and transpersonal psychology, as well as what can be called "non-ordinary" states of consciousness (NOSCs). Notably, there are no current models or frameworks for working with NOSC. This is particularly significant considering the renewed interest in psychedelics, spirituality, psi phenomena, and other paranormal and exceptional experiences. This model neatly offers a syncretic framework for working with these non-ordinary psychospiritual states as an extension of normal human development. Moreover, as a meta-model, other models and theories can be usefully organized within its structure.

The circuits, briefly, are as follows:

THE LOWER CIRCUITS:
PERSONAL EGOIC HUMAN DEVELOPMENT

Circuit 0—Prenatal Intelligence: (This circuit was not included in the original 8-Circuit Model of Consciousness) Prenatal and perinatal experiences and influences; Stanislav Grof's Basic Perinatal Matrices

Circuit 1—Somatic Intelligence: Basic needs of survival, physical security and safety; fear and fright; attachment style; adverse childhood events

Circuit 2—Emotional Intelligence: Emotional needs; your role in the social hierarchy/territorial politics; power dynamics in relationships (docile /submissive vs. assertive/dominant); autonomy vs. dependence

Circuit 3—Symbolic Intelligence: Logic, symbolic thought, language /semantics, writing; dexterity; mathematics; development of representational mental maps; cognitive processes; executive functions

Circuit 4—Social Intelligence: Social groups and expectations; cultural norms and morals; conformity, shame and guilt; tribal behaviors, religious and other rites of passage into adulthood; sexuality, morality and superego development; social proscriptions and prescriptions

THE UPPER CIRCUITS:
NON-ORDINARY STATES OF CONSCIOUSNESS &
TRANSPERSONAL EXPERIENCES

Circuit 5—Aesthetic Intelligence: Pursuit of pleasure for its own sake; states of "flow," "awe," "bliss"; rapturous and ecstatic states; hedonic engineering; eco-consciousness

Circuit 6—Meta-Intelligence: Conscious and intentional self-transformation: metaprogramming (conscious and intentional deprogramming and reimprinting of yourself in accordance with more internally /transpersonally-defined constructs of Self); awareness of influences and conditioning on personality and the sense of Self

Circuit 7—Collective Intelligence: Inter-generational hereditary /genetic memory and trauma; epigenetics, archetypes, synchronicity; astral plane/astral projection; experiences with non-physical/discarnate entities, paranormal and psi experiences, telepathy; "psychoid space"

Circuit 8—Unitive Intelligence: Non-dual states; ego dissolution; dream states; near-death experiences (NDE); out-of-body experiences (OBE); feeling of oneness with the universe or "God" (henosis)

COMPLEXITY VS. HIERARCHY

It is important to note that the terms "lower" and "higher" circuits are used for simplicity, and (to be blunt) the lack of more precise terms. ***It does not imply any form of hierarchy among the circuits.*** While the personal egoic stages in Circuits 1–4 tend to develop linearly, once established they each become important parts of Self that remain in play and are accessible to those aware of how to do so. The "upper" circuits that encompass non-ordinary and transpersonal states may happen in any order (non-linearly). They, along with the first four circuits, are discussed in order of increasing complexity and broadness of scope, with none being inherently "better" than another. Each is considered to hold a valuable role in the human experience.

THE NEURON MODEL OF INTELLIGENCE

The 8-Circuit Model material and this Workbook references what is known as the neuron model of intelligence which is based on the way that neurons in the human nervous system operate in three main stages:

- **"Absorb" (Signal Reception):** information is received from another neuron
- **"Integrate" (Signal Integration/Interpretation):** information becomes coherent in the cell body
- **"Transmit" (Signal Transmission):** information is passed onto the next neuron

Neurological Imprinting & "Critical Periods" of Development

This is the concept that life events at particular stages of development set patterns that tend to continue to play out throughout your lifetime. This seems to happen in very narrow windows of development, and what happens in each of these windows essentially becomes "hard-wired" into the nervous system and psyche. This establishes an "imprint" (i.e., an internalized "belief structure") about a particular aspect of the world that, without significant self-work, remains unlikely to change. The term "neuroarcheology" has been used to describe the degree that events and experiences have on the developing brain based on several factors: intensity, nature, pattern, duration, and the resulting strengths or deficits from these experiences.

"Reality Tunnels"

Each individual has a unique human experience, lived through their individual nervous system, that has been constructed by their own past, background, education, traumas, and life paths. From these experiences, the development of your personal model of the world and how it works (your "reality tunnel") have been (mostly unconsciously) influenced. Some of this structuring of reality has served us well, and may continue to do so. Other aspects could use some refinement or change.

This concept has been reinvented in contemporary times. Neuroscientists Heather Berlin and Christof Koch co-host *Science of Perception Box*, exploring how the brain constructs lived reality through filters like memory, emotion, bias, and conditioning. The show draws on the Perception Box framework developed by Elizabeth Koch, which describes how each person's "box" shapes what they notice, believe, and assume is true. This maps closely onto Leary and Wilson's idea of a reality tunnel: both describe perception as a subjective model of the world, and emphasize that growth often comes from recognizing the filter and learning to loosen it.

Much of this Workbook aims at making your model of reality and subconscious processes more conscious; that is, allowing for more intentional and accessible change or refinement.

Treadmilling

Treadmilling happens when you operate narrowly within a particular circuit. If you are treadmilling, you may become rigidly locked within the confines of those parts of yourself relating to that circuit, while ignoring or neglecting other parts of your Self. It can occur by any of the following:

- Failure to sufficiently integrate your experience
- Lack of communication from not linking experiences with others
- Absorbing more data than there is time or energy to integrate

Another way to think of this is that certain material/experiences may become "stuck" or "constipated," and not properly "digested."

Shocks & Anchors

We explore vertical relationships between the circuits as follows, with the lower circuits acting as "anchors" for upper circuit "shocks", and conversely, the upper circuits acting as catalysts of change for lower circuit imbalances:

- Circuits 1 & 5: relationship of safety and security; anchors ecstasy and bliss shocks
- Circuits 2 & 6: relationship of power and control; anchors uncertainty and freedom shocks

- Circuits 3 & 7: relationship of sanity and communication; anchors unity and synchronicity shocks
- Circuits 4 & 8: relationship of community and belonging; anchors impermanence and death shocks

"Shocks" are experiences that risk destabilizing the "anchors" which are foundational experiences that ground yourself within your body, emotions, mind, and community (established within Circuits 1–4); they may result in a loss of a sense of purpose or context. The circuits exist as different but simultaneous parts of ourselves that can influence how others are operating. For instance, a sudden Circuit 7 experience may "shock" the nervous system into a vastly more complex state, and may destabilize your Circuit 3 models of compartmentalization and rationalized, logic-based models of reality. If this happens you may feel as if you are losing your grip on the Circuit 3 anchor of sanity; you may feel that you are losing your mind! In a sense, you very well may be—at least your mind as you've previously experienced it within the limitations of pre-transpersonal consciousness. These shocks can also be helpful with respect to re-imprinting the lower circuits and breaking free from rigid or restrictive imprints or thought patterns. Conversely, healthy and balanced lower circuits can have an anchoring effect that allows for safe exploration of the upper circuits.

METAPROGRAMMING

One goal of this Workbook is to explore approaches that have the potential to change detrimental or rigid imprints, belief systems, and deleterious effects they may have. Exploring these negative imprints, and working to alter them, may be referred to as "re-imprinting," or per the work of Dr. John Lilly, "metaprogramming." This may not be a straightforward process. You must be at a place that allows for vulnerability and flexibility, as well as one that allows you to process and integrate the information. This Workbook offers a practical guide to facilitate metaprogramming. If you are interested in understanding this concept more deeply, we have explored metaprogramming in more detail throughout the Guide.

CHAPTER GOALS

- Gain understanding about reality tunnels and how they may influence your perception of the world
- Gain insight into how strongly events earlier in your life may have set a tone for how you process information and experiences now
- Consider the idea that every person has a different experience of the world, and how these experiences shape and influence the way you view and interpret the world. Imagine being born into a different set of circumstances and having a different set of life experiences; imagine how this might affect who you are, your beliefs, behaviors, etc.

REFLECTIONS

How do you define intelligence?

____

____

____

____

____

____

Using your definition of intelligence, how would you go about increasing your intelligence?

____

____

____

____

____

____

What are some life events, experiences, or belief structures that have played a role in your definition or view of reality? Of Self? Of intelligence?

____

____

____

____

____

____

Can you think of a life event you would consider a "shock"—one that shook you or the way you think about yourself and/or the world? This might include a religious, spiritual, or mystical experience; an experience where you felt a great deal of awe, inspiration, or elation; or a connection with something more than yourself (e.g., another person/other people, a community, the Earth, the cosmos). How would you describe that feeling?

Reflect on any life experiences you've had that didn't make sense with the way you understand the world/reality; or seemed too weird to be true; and/or felt indescribable?

Can you think of a life event in which you felt "spaced-out," disoriented, or ungrounded? Did you find anything that has been helpful in pulling you back into a more present, embodied, or relaxed state?

Make a short list of actions you do or have done that help you reflect on yourself and your thoughts? How often do you do these activities?

____

____

____

____

Have you ever felt "stuck in a loop" with your thoughts or emotions? Have you noticed anything that can be helpful in breaking this loop? Can you think of anything new that might be helpful?

____

____

____

____

____

____

CHAPTER 2

CIRCUIT 0: VALENCE JUMPING; THE PRENATAL & PERINATAL MATRICES

CHAPTER SUMMARY

The developing fetus exists in a passive state of receptivity, interacting only within the confines of the womb. Every experience, to some degree, is filtered through the mother's nervous system. Because of this, the mother's experiences during this time have a big influence on the child's development. Everything from diet, exposure to stress, drug and alcohol misuse, prescription drugs, and pollution can all shape fetal development, and may have a continued effect into adulthood.

A mother's behavior directly influences gene expression in neural growth, including a higher risk of chronic diseases such as diabetes, obesity, and heart disease, as well as a shorter lifespan.

Early life adversity also plays a critical role in development by altering DNA. This can increase the risk of mental health concerns, and can impact hormonal development and stress response.

The following is a summary of what Dr. Stanislav Grof referred to as the Basic Perinatal Matrices (BPM) of the fetal experience. Grof, in his work with LSD-assisted psychotherapy, noted that people would have "re-experiencing" events in which they would seem to relive prenatal or perinatal experiences, sometimes with great—and very specific—detail.

Matrix	Phase	Experience
I	Gestation before labor	Oceanic oneness; heavenly, unless there is trauma, in which case it can be experienced as "poisonous womb"
II	Labor prior to cervix opening	Hellish, frustrated, and in despair
III	Cervix has opened	Passion and anger; animalistic themes—"Through tooth and claw, one must survive"
IV	Delivery	Ego-death, conquered tribulations, liberation

Neurobiology

The greater part of neural development occurs during the prenatal period at an average rate of about 250,000(!) nerve cells per minute throughout pregnancy. However, many of these cells die off soon after birth (a process called "pruning"), so this makes prenatal brain development a critical time period.

Chapter Lessons

- Many factors can influence a developing human being in the womb
- A pregnant mother's experiences and lifestyle choices can have a significant impact on the development of a child
- While in the womb, the child's nervous and hormone systems can be directly impacted by stress to either the mother or child
- These can influence, and have a continued impact into adulthood and through the entire life

- Through re-experiencing perinatal experiences in altered states of consciousness, it is possible to heal traumas that happened during this stage of development

CIRCUIT 0 IMBALANCES

- Chronic "background" anxiety with no object
- Difficulty initiating (projects, relationships, transitions)
- Feeling out-of-sync with life
- Existential guilt ("I shouldn't be here")
- Sensitivity to sudden change or interruption
- Difficulty resting into support even when safe

REFLECTIONS

Core theme: Protection/support vs. toxicity

Imprint age: Conception → fetal development → birth → immediate postnatal transition.

Mantra: *"I'm allowed to be here." "Nothing is required for me to be here." "I do not have to earn existence."*

Are you a first child or had your mother had prior childbirths?

What do you know of your mother's experiences during pregnancy? Are you aware of any major life events or stressors that occurred while you were in utero? Do you know about your mother's diet and lifestyle while pregnant?

How much do you know about your birth? Were you born prematurely, on time, or late? Where were you born (hospital, home, elsewhere)? Was it a vaginal birth or cesarean section? Was it a natural birth or were painkillers and/or other drugs administered? Who was present (doctors and nurses, a midwife/doula, others)?

Are you aware of any complications or birth traumas that may have occurred during your birth?

ACTION STEPS

The following can be helpful for exploring or recreating the prenatal experience, and may be useful for re-programming negative perinatal experiences. It may also be helpful to regulate your nervous system—specifically the autonomic nervous system—by recreating a womb-like environment that is warm, safe, and supportive. Pay attention to sensations that may come up, and how this feels within your body. Simulating a perinatal experience can may be done in several ways:

- Sensory deprivation/floatation tank: warm, high-salt-content water
- Weighted and/or heated blanket(s): create a safe and nurturing space by swathing yourself in a warm security blanket
- A comfort bubble or blanket fort: surround yourself with pillows, stuffed animals, or other soft, warm, and comforting objects

- People: don't just hug or cuddle, but let yourself be fully held and embraced; or if it feels comforting and safe, allow a trusted person (or people) to put their body weight onto you
- The inner fetus: buy (or create) a baby doll and put it under your shirt, pretending that you are pregnant with yourself. Briefly visualize and experience each of Grof's stages, imagining a loving, healing, nurturing connection and environment between "mother" and your fetus Self. After you give birth to yourself, be sure to immediately imagine breastfeeding the newborn you, and lovingly look into the newborn's eyes, which in real-life would stimulate the release of oxytocin, the "pair-binding" or "love" hormone. Make a vow to always love and protect this perfect being (i.e., YOU!)

Either along with the above, or on its own, sit and listen to the sound of a human heartbeat for several minutes. Pay attention to how this feels, as well as any emotions that you may notice.

Rhythmic Regulation Practice

Circuit 0 entrains through rhythm (like a mother's heartbeat). Choose one of the following (or experiment with your own related ideas):

- Go on a walk, slowly walking with breath-step synchronization
- Rocking motion (swing, rocking chair)
- Low-frequency shamanic drumming or heartbeat audio

No visualization is required for this exercise, just pure feeling. Allow your mind to empty as you lean into the feeling, *"Nothing is required for me to be here."*

Pure Presence Meditation

Set aside 10–15 minutes where the only intention is pure presence and acceptance of being, without expectation or pressure. If this feels too long, honor where you're at and start with whatever feels doable. Even starting with just one minute is okay. You can incrementally increase the amount of time spent in meditation over time.

This mediation is not about goal-setting, insight, or healing. The focus is about the underlying imprint of unconditional presence and feeling welcome in your body and environment. Allow your nervous system to tune everything else out and just *be*.

Delayed Response Training

Practice pausing for a moment before responding to stimuli (e.g., messages, environmental noises, interpersonal requests), even if only for 2–5 seconds. This helps to counteract the primordial peri-natal shock pattern of birth in which you were abruptly forced to react to the unexpected traumatic disruption from your warm, dark, and shielded in utero environment.

Safe Dependency "Microdoses"

Circuit 0 needs experiences of support without obligation. Some examples:

- Being physically supported (massage, bodywork, float tank).
- Accepting gifts or asking for something small and letting it be given.
- Sitting against a wall or person and doing nothing, just feeling the support of your body.

Try to think of some of your own safe dependency microdoses. The key is *receiving without exchange*, and learning to feel worthy of this experience.

Circuit 0 Re-Imprinting Meditation: The Womb

For some, re-enacting the process of being birthed can be impactful. Doing so in a safe space can help soften or re-imprint negative or difficult early-life imprints.

If you can, ask someone who was present during the time you were in the womb, and find out anything you can about the conditions of that phase of your life: what was your mother's situation, your mother's nutritional intake, any drug or alcohol use, the living situation, any major external stressors, support systems, etc. This information can be helpful in identifying negative imprints and guiding your healing experience.

You may want to record this guided journey, speaking with a soft, soothing voice with calming, ambient music playing quietly in the background. Or perhaps you have a female support person whose voice you find soothing who would be willing to record it for you. This may be combined with the Threshold Ritual that simulates the birthing process; it is described immediately after the following meditation.

Dim the lights and imagine yourself as a developing fetus. Wrap yourself in a warm, comfortable blanket (ideally, thick, soft, and weighted) and lie in a fetal position; or, if possible, perform this exercise floating in an isolation tank.

Use your breath to regulate your nervous system, inhaling gently and naturally, with a slightly longer exhale.

Let your body soften and settle without effort. Imagine being held by gravity itself—held within a warm, calm fluid in pitch darkness.

As you deepen into feelings of safety and containment, repeat the following mantra internally:

"Nothing is required for me to be here."

Feel this through every cell in your body. Feel this penetrate the deepest layer of your core and throughout the very essence of your being.

This may feel dysregulating at first if there is deep trauma. You may become tearful, resistant, or incredulous of healing. Trust your innermost healer and truest sense of self, and stay there until the body settles on its own, as you gently repeat the mantra, *"Nothing is required for me to be here."*

Allow yourself to shift into a state of soft, empty presence—no thoughts, no feelings, no identity, no memory, no expectations, no explanations—just pure, unbothered presence.

Once you relax into this state, gently feel your conscious mind return to your body.

> In this space, you are supported safely...
> You are wanted and welcomed...
> You know nothing but pure being... Resting in pure comfort...
> Feel this wholeness with your entire being.

Stay in this state of eternal, oceanic consciousness for as long as you are able to, integrating the message, *"Nothing is required for me to be here"* into the very center of the core of your being.

Sense the simplest facts:

> You are here now. You exist. You are included.
> No role. No task. No becoming. You don't need to improve anything.
> Just this quiet allowance: It is s*afe to be here.*

Stay in this space for as long as you feel necessary. Do not try to interpret anything until later. Just allow yourself to be fully present within your body...in the safety of this loving womb...knowing you are perfect just as you are.

THRESHOLD RITUAL

Dim the lights and stand near an open doorway. Pause before crossing, feeling your feet stable on the ground. Cross slowly. If you have a trusted support person, you may want to lie on the floor and ask him or her to gently push or pull you through the threshold, and then greet you with love on the other side (e.g., holding you, petting your head or back). If you don't have a trusted support person available, you may want to use a stuffed animal, weighted blanket, or just sitting against the wall, feeling the support of the floor and wall on your body.

This gently retrains the system around transition safety, which is a core peri-natal theme. Repeat this daily for one week.

CIRCUIT 0 INTEGRATION QUESTIONS
WEEKLY REFLECTION

- What did I learn about my earliest imprinting this week?
- How has my sense of basic existence shifted?
- What practices most supported my Circuit 0 activation?
- Where do I still feel a core sense of threat, emptiness, or non-belonging?
- What does my nervous system need to feel held and allowed?
- How is Circuit 0 health affecting my higher circuits?

CHAPTER 3

CIRCUIT 1: SURVIVAL, SAFETY & COMFORT

CHAPTER SUMMARY

In early life, basic survival needs may seem like the only drives we have: Above all else, a living organism must establish how to regulate itself enough to survive. A wide range of patterns of illnesses can develop as a reaction to unmet physical and emotional needs. First circuit survival needs tend to be more *felt* within the body than *thought about* within the mind.

During early development, the newborn does not experience itself as separate from the primary caregiver, but rather as an undifferentiated extension. If a primary caregiver isn't physically or emotionally present, the loss felt by the child is profound. It could be argued that no other trauma exists that creates such a deeply rippling effect through the psyche, and continues to have an impact on many levels throughout the rest of life.

IMPRINTING SAFETY

Circuit 1 (C-1) dynamics are typically imprinted within the first six months of life, and may even be impacted prenatally. During this time, the primary caregiver is a key factor in determining whether the child takes on a "positive" or "negative" imprint or perspective on issues of safety and openness to interactions with the environment. The imprint is a general "forward-backward" program—moving either forward *toward* experiences felt as safe, cuddly, nurturing, or sociable, or *backward* away from experiences felt as dangerous, noxious, cruel, or destructive.

This period of development coincides with Piaget's sensorimotor stage (0–2 years), in which infants learn mostly through trial and error, relying on reflexes, and eventually changing or controlling them to adapt to the world. We are relational creatures: when a child feels safe and secure, their social engagement system (i.e., face, eyes, mouth, and middle ear) and heart work coherently, allowing the child to interact with others. Facial expression, eye contact, tone of voice, and hand movements are how interactions, connections, and the emotions of others are processed.

Compensatory Imprinting

The biological drive for nourishment, comfort, and security are so strong that the child, in the absence of an effective source, may seek out and establish a replacement. This may be another person (or even a member of a different species), or a need-fulfilling object. A child may form a compensatory imprint such as a favorite person they never want to be apart from, a favorite toy that's taken everywhere, or a blanket they are never without. The object becomes even more likely to be imprinted if it has some association with an historically nurturing figure. The body's primary initiative is to be felt deeply, and it will go to great lengths to make sure that is achieved.

Adverse Childhood Experiences (ACEs) & Early Life Negative Imprints

Birth trauma, traumatic events during vulnerable periods of imprinting, or traumatic child-rearing conditions can create a negative imprint. A 1997 study on adverse child experiences (ACEs) by the Centers for Disease Control and Prevention (CDC) showed that more than half of the participants reported some significant adverse and potentially destabilizing effect in young childhood. A 2020 review found "almost two thirds of youth experience significant adverse events no matter where they reside across the world." The World Health Organization (WHO) estimates that child maltreatment is responsible for almost a quarter of mental health syndromes.

The ten primary ACEs identified in the study were grouped into three categories:

- **Abuse:** emotional, physical, or sexual
- **Neglect**: emotional, physical
- **Household challenges:** domestic abuse or violence; substance abuse; mental illness; parental separation or divorce; incarcerated parent or relative

This study did not include other adverse experiences such as bullying, community violence, natural disasters, war, displacement, poverty/economic hardship, oppression, and racism, any of which can also contribute.

Trauma can show up as a wide range of body-mind symptoms. The cumulative effects of ACEs are considered significant risk factors for several leading causes of death in adults including: COPD, asthma, obesity, kidney disease, stroke, coronary heart disease, cancer, diabetes, and substance abuse as well as poor general health, sleep disturbances, increased absences from school, learning difficulties, ADHD, autism spectrum disorder, and various violent and suicide-related behaviors.

CO-REGULATION & DEVELOPMENT OF SELF-REGULATION/DYSREGULATION

It has been argued that the single most important discovery scientists have made about the early years of development is that by co-regulating, a child more readily develops their ability to self-regulate. Moreover, child-led play has been emphasized as a central, leading role in the development of self-regulation and executive functioning skills.

During early development, your entire existence revolves around meeting basic survival needs and the sensory exploration of the world around you. The most fulfilling of all of these needs is the mother-child bond during the act of breastfeeding, where you are not only receiving essential nourishment, but sensory fulfillment as well—two beings co-regulating one another's nervous systems. The safer and more nourishing the infant's environment is, the more positive their neurological imprint will be, and as such, they are more likely to develop a more expansive overall view of the world.

Five Key Domains of Self-Regulation

- **Biological:** Too much visual or noise stimulation, insufficient exercise, having to be too still, cluttered classroom, physical illness
- **Emotional:** Both positive (over-excitement) and negative (fear and anger), anxiety, routine changes
- **Cognitive**: Trouble processing certain information—organizing thoughts, time constraints, interruptions
- **Social:** Trouble understanding the effect of your behavior on others and understanding social cues; bullying
- **Prosocial:** Difficulty coping with others' stress, feelings of injustice, being late, empathy and sympathy

The state of arousal and the amount of stimulation provided or sought out by the young child also has a direct effect on behavior and the ability to develop self-regulation:

- **Overstimulation:** Can affect executive functions like self-regulation, impulse control, working memory, planning, problem-solving, concentration, and learning; leaving little space for self-talk; can cause hyperactivity, sensory overload. Neurodivergent children are particularly vulnerable
- **Understimulation:** Can cause passivity in children; self-limiting behaviors; does not ignite children's innate curiosity; children will not be stretched or challenged. This can lead to a state of hypo-arousal, which can relate to dissociation, zoning out, flat affect, feeling empty, numb or dead inside, general lethargy, hypervigilance, disconnection between thoughts, feelings, and behaviors, and a separation between mind and body

Neophilia

If your needs are attended to enough to create a positive C-1 imprint, you will tend to have a greater ability and desire to explore the world with confidence, bravery, and natural curiosity. But, if you imprint negatively, you will tend more toward timidity, fear of new situations, and withdrawal; the world may become seen as a harsh, hostile, and frightening place. Later in life, this withdrawal can also manifest as rigid ideologies about particular groups of humans.

The Autonomic Nervous System & Autonomic Regulation

At this early stage, the most basic instinctual drives for survival are at the forefront, with "guttural" reactionary responses to the environment determining actions. The portion of the brain where these in-the-moment instincts seem to derive from is often referred to—in the triune model of the brain—as the "reptilian" brain, "R-complex," or the ponto-medullary reticular formation (PMRF). This consists mostly of the brainstem, midbrain, cerebellum, and components of the autonomic nervous system (ANS). These brain structures regulate the body's automatic functions and drives, including eating, excreting, and maintaining sleep/circadian rhythms. Other autonomic functions—including hormonal regulation of temperature, growth rate, and metabolism—also fall into this category.

Scarcity Mentality & Letting Things Go

The tendency for the body to hold onto and store more of its nutritional intake is a means of maintaining survival resources. If you are in a situation where basic food needs may not be met, you will have assurance of stored emergency resources, and thus be more likely to survive. Those with a heavy first circuit imprint may also experience similar tendencies in other aspects of their adult life. These may include clinging to people or material possessions—often in the hope that these will offer a sense of survival security or fulfillment of an internal longing, a sense of emptiness, or the feeling that something is missing. Such a person may become fixated on food, shelter, money, and/or self-preservation—gathering beyond necessity. Hoarding is an extreme example of this. Over-consumption, by any means, whether physical possessions or eating, can be an attempt to fill this felt void or deal with a negative imprint.

RELATIONSHIP TO THE BODY

Because your body acts as the primary mechanism of this circuit, a negative imprint can also result in a negative perception of your body. "Body trashing," "not feeling comfortable in your own skin," or the perception that the body is somehow "bad" can all come about. You may ignore the body's needs for nourishment, or for somatic feelings to be felt deeply. With enough negligence, physical symptoms will develop; or you may become accident prone in a type of self-fulfilling prophecy. A healthy first circuit recognizes and listens to the needs of the body and the fundamental role it plays in growth and development.

Body language—the ways we use our bodies—is directly interpreted by others and often communicates more information than verbal exchange. If your body projects a presence of safety or confidence, this is picked up by others, allowing them to feel at ease.

FEAR & INTEGRITY—EXPANSION & CONTRACTION

Bringing your breath to a more natural rhythm is a tool utilized by a variety of body-based and yogic approaches. Fear and first circuit imbalances can develop fundamental breathing restrictions. Fear creates a full-body response, and plays a significant role in C-1 processing; thus, it's important to attune with your somatic feelings, and work through/release them to address any imbalances. To work with your body, you need to be able to deeply feel it and to process/integrate sensory information. Different types of sensory information include: kinesthetic (tactile/physical activity), proprioceptive (sense of your body and movements in physical space), and interoceptive (awareness of your body's internal state).

Integrity is also a major influential component of the biosurvival circuit. The inability or ability to keep your word, especially to yourself, can negatively or positively reinforce the state of the first circuit, respectively. Saying what you mean and meaning what you say reinforces safety and the ability to trust yourself and the world.

NEUROCEPTION & POLYVAGAL THEORY

Neuroception is a term that describes how the nervous system distinguishes whether situations or people are safe, dangerous, or life-threatening while also influencing our social or defensive behaviors. Polyvagal theory describes three stages in the development of the autonomic nervous system:

- Immobilization ("freeze")
- Mobilization ("fight or flight")
- Social communication/engagement

Mobilization is explored more in Circuit 2. Social engagement is explored more in Circuit 4.

The immobilization (aka "freeze") response in the face of threat is expressed in other mammals as "death feigning"—fainting goats are an example. In humans there is a behavioral shutdown, often followed by muscular weakness. Heart rate and breathing slow as blood pressure drops. Pain threshold also increases.

ATTACHMENT THEORY

Attachment theory can provide a useful model of early childhood C-1 imprinting. This theory builds from the foundation that early attachment behavior is mostly driven by seeking proximity to an attachment figure—generally, the primary caregiver—in stressful situations. Infants from about six months to two years of age become attached to adults who are sensitive and responsive in interactions with them, or those who remain consistent during this period. Patterns of communication between caregiver and infant lead to relationship dynamics that create an internalized model of security. When patterns of communication are consistent, predictable, and filled with "repairs" in the event of inevitable "ruptures," this model of security becomes established.

Four categories of attachment styles have been proposed:

- **Secure:** the child feels nurtured, safe, and secure (this tends to develop into a secure attachment style in adults)
- **Anxious-avoidant:** the child is unresponsive or indifferent to the parent (this tends to develop into a dismissive-avoidant attachment style in adults)
- **Anxious-ambivalent:** the child shows clingy behavior at first, then rejects attempts by the caregiver as care cannot be consistently relied upon (this tends to develop into an anxious-preoccupied attachment style in adults)
- **Disorganized:** the child experiences both excessive (anxious) approach and excessive avoidance or withdrawal (this tends to develop into a fearful avoidant attachment style in adults)

NEUROBIOLOGY

There are short, brain-growth stages within the first year of life.

New synapse growth is highly prolific in the first five years of life. At birth, each neuron in the cerebral cortex has approximately 2,500 synapses. By age three the number is about 15,000—about twice that of the average adult brain. This growth depends on opportunities for play, exploration, and communication with others. Repetition strengthens the existing connections.

Between three and 10 months of age, the cerebellum matures to facilitate the activation and control of motor actions and monitoring of errors in movement. If the child does not already have enough sensory experiences or support structure around, these new connections will build onto a less than optimal set so the new controls and their functioning will not be optimal.

Stress has a wide-ranging effect on neurological and immunological development. Stressors such as fear/anxiety, social aggression, and social/emotional avoidance raise the stress hormone cortisol and often results in irritability, fear, and withdrawal from others, and predisposes the individual to chronic immunological and other health/mental health conditions.

Childhood trauma seems to directly impact brain development: overall decreased brain size, less efficient processing, impaired stress response, and changes in gene expression. Cognition can be affected with impaired readiness to learn and solve problems; language delays; poor concentration; and poor academic achievement.

CHAPTER LESSONS

- Safety and comfort
- Neuroception
- Nurturing
- Relationship with the body
- Exploration vs. avoidance
- Kinesthetic and tactile information
- Autonomic regulation
- Expansion and contraction
- The role of breathing
- Fear and the freeze response
- Attachment styles
- Co-regulation and self-regulation

GOALS

- Consider/explore how early life circumstances may continue to play out in your daily life and your perception/interpretation of reality
- Recognize potential C-1 disharmonies or imbalances

- Explore multiple models (attachment theory/polyvagal theory, etc.) and compare similarities within the C-1 landscape
- Consider ways that improve or maximize your Circuit 1 intelligence

Qualities of Circuit 1 Dynamics

Balanced Circuit 1 Energy

- Centered, grounded
- Friendly, affectionate
- Healthy; ample physical energy
- Ability to manifest abundance
- Ability to express needs without doing harm
- Ability to care for yourself while respecting others' needs
- Sexual: affectionate; able to trust and be vulnerable; body sensuality

Excessive Circuit 1 Energy "Too Far Forward"

- Egotistic, critical, aggressive
- Forthright, frank, firm, sarcastic
- Domineering, punitive
- Greedy, hoarding, overconsumption
- Possible eating disorders
- Difficulty letting go
- Addicted to wealth/accumulation/consumption
- Sexual: indiscriminate, focus purely genital, nervous; possible sadism

Deficient Circuit 1 Energy "Too Far Backward"

- Chronic fear and victimization
- Feels at the mercy of the environment; unable to stand on your own
- Lacks confidence; weakness
- Overly agreeable/cooperative
- Feels spacey or unfocused

- Unable to achieve goals
- Self-destructive, self-harm, possibly suicidal
- Denial or anxiety around the body and bodily sensations
- Low sense of your body (interoceptive and proprioceptive awareness)
- Possible eating disorders
- Sexual: feels unlovable, fears abandonment; low libido; possible masochism and other similar fetishes

REFLECTIONS

Core theme: Survival, safety, trust, embodied existence

Imprint age: Around 6 months through ~2 years

Mantra: *"I am safe in my body." "My needs will be met." "I have enough." "I am worthy." "I will be okay."*

How easily do you let things go (e.g., belongings/emotions/grudges)?

List personal adverse child experiences (ACEs) with as much detail as you find helpful to reflect on. Note: While it is important to be present with difficult emotions, it is also important to know your limits. If this triggers a traumatic response, don't push yourself—you can stop at any time if you feel overwhelmed.

How do you feel your childhood experiences around comfort, needs, security, and safety influence your current worldview?

How do you feel your childhood experiences around comfort, needs, security, and safety influence how you approach new situations?

How do you feel your childhood experiences around comfort, needs, security, and safety influence your actions/choices/interactions?

When have you felt most safe? What does this feel like in your body?

When have you felt fully nourished? What does this feel like in your body?

When have you felt as though your needs have been fully supported? What does this feel like in your body?

When have you felt "fulfilled"—fully filled to the brim? What does this feel like in your body?

When you were younger, did you have any comfort items? How attached to these items were you? How attached to these items are you now?

Who or what are your comfort items/safe people—both in childhood and now?

How often do you feel anxious? What does that feel like in your body?

What are your biggest fears? Are these rooted in something you're aware of?

What makes your heart happy?

When was the last time you felt a childlike wonder?

When was the last time you felt a freeze or startle response? Is this something you experience often? Would you guess it occurs more often or less often than most people? Do you startle easily?

List any personal triggers you are aware of for these freeze or startle responses.

Are you aware of where and how you store stress or emotions within your body? Are there areas that tend to be very tight, rigid, or closed off? Reflect on why these particular areas may be this way for you. You may even notice mythopoetic themes (e.g., nausea when you "can't stomach something," or tightness of the shoulders if you feel you "carry the weight of the world" on your shoulders).

What rejuvenation or grounding practices do you enjoy or find works well for you? See the above list of C-1 activities for ideas.

How does reading and working through this material feel to you?

Try to identify people (real or fictional) who embody quintessential C-1 characteristics. What are their strengths and flaws?

What would the world look like if Circuit 1 was the primary circuit people operated from?

ACTION STEPS

Notice how your body relates to rest, support, and presence. Do you allow yourself to fully settle, or do you remain subtly braced, guarded, or hypervigilant? When nothing is required of you, does your body soften, or does it search for something to manage?

Rather than trying to feel safe, begin by observing how your body feels in neutral moments.

Ask yourself:

What happens in my body when I stop doing?
Where do I hold tension as a precaution rather than a response?
What signals of comfort or fatigue do I ignore?

Repair at this level doesn't come from insight or verbal reassurance, but from repeated experiences of being supported, valued, and validated without expectation or demand of anything in return. Repair at this stage is often nonverbal at the deepest somatic levels, allowing your body to learn that it can rest in safety and feel secure that your most basic survival needs will be met and tended to.

Some examples of activities that allow you to feel the body more fully, or experience sensations or perceptions of safety and having basic needs met may include:

- Cooking and consciously immersing yourself in a fulfilling meal
- Epsom salt bath while consciously paying attention to the sounds and rhythms of the body including heartbeat, breath, digestion, etc.
- Activities that regulate or stimulate the vagus nerve; i.e., gargling water, humming, "aum"ing
- Grounding in nature or gardening (horticulture therapy)
- Big hugs; cuddling or being held securely
- Massage—particularly head, shoulders, feet, or abdomen ("hara")
- Floatation/isolation tanks
- Resting/sleeping—adequate rest allows you to "recharge" and feel more safe/secure
- Trying to look at the world through the eyes of an infant in constant wonder and receptivity
- Breathing exercises (e.g., blowing bubbles)
- Having a cozy place to crawl into and relax
- Tapping/acupressure
- Picturing a happy place or favorite activity
- Naming five favorite things
- Breathing a favorite or soothing scent (aromatherapy)
- Identifying emotions with an adult (nurturing figure)
- Being in nature/outside
- Listening to soothing music
- Repeating positive affirmations
- Autonomic regulation techniques
- Trauma Release Exercises (TRE)
- Eye Movement Desensitization and Reprocessing (EMDR) therapy

- Circuit 1 yoga
- Abdominal or perineal breathing
- Intentional processing of or therapy around healing relational wounds, especially those with caregivers
- Modeling of appropriate attachment
- Grounding work/meditations
- Define personal safety

INVENTORY OF UNMET C-1 NEEDS

Make a list of unmet C-1 needs disguised as habits (e.g., scrolling = touch hunger, overworking = safety anxiety, hoarding = fear of scarcity, excessive alcohol consumption = connection hunger). Choose a non-negotiable in the next exercise (the *30-Day Body Reliability Agreement*) that counterbalances the habit that addresses this need.

30-DAY BODY RELIABILITY AGREEMENT

Pick one non-negotiable daily act that proves your body will be cared for (e.g., go to bed at the same time each night, or go for a daily walk at a set time). Choose something that you can realistically commit to as consistency matters more than quality. Ideally, it should meet the need(s) identified in the previous exercise.

GROUNDING PRACTICES

To establish daily practices that activate Circuit 1 health, choose 2–3 practices to do daily for at least one week:

PHYSICAL GROUNDING

- Walk barefoot on earth for 10 minutes
- Full body stretching/yoga for 20 minutes
- Conscious eating (one meal fully present, no distractions)

Breath Work

- 4-7-8 breathing (inhale 4, hold 7, exhale 8) for 4 cycles
- Belly breathing while lying down, 10 minutes
- Humming/toning to activate vagal nerve

Environmental

- Create a "safety nest" space in your home
- Organize one area that feels chaotic
- Ensure 8 hours of sleep in total silence and darkness
- Remove one source of chronic stress/threat

Mindful Check-ins & Resets

Purpose: Return to parasympathetic rest state throughout the day

Practice

Set 5–8 alarms throughout your day. When the alarm sounds:

- **STOP** whatever you're doing
- **SENSE** your environment—what do you see, hear, smell?
- **SAFETY CHECK**—Am I actually in danger right now?
- **SOFTEN**—Relax the jaw, shoulders, belly, or any other tension in the body
- **SIGH**—A big exhale releasing tension
- **SMILE**—A slight upturn of the lips signals safety to nervous system

Journal After 1 Week

- How often were you in sympathetic activation unnecessarily?
- What triggers false alarms in your system?
- Did this practice increase baseline safety?

Simple Re-Imprinting Visualization

- Close your eyes and imagine your infant self

- hat does this baby need to feel completely safe?
- As your adult self, provide this safety
- Hold the baby, rock them, assure them they are safe and welcome
- Notice sensations in your body as you do this

CIRCUIT 1 RE-IMPRINTING MEDITATION: CAREGIVER & INFANT ATTUNEMENT

You may wish to record this meditation in a soft, steady voice, or have a trusted person who evokes feelings of safety and security record it for you. Dim the lights and lie down comfortably wrapped in a warm blanket. It can be helpful to work with an inner-child doll, stuffed animal, or soft object in this meditation; if you have one, hold it lovingly as you would a baby.

Begin by gently regulating your breath—inhale naturally, exhale slightly longer than the inhale. Take a few intentional breaths, allow your body to settle comfortably.

First, feel yourself as the caregiver:

Notice the weight of your body, the steadiness of your spine, the warmth in your hands. You are grounded here in loving presence.

Gently hold the infant in your arms (your inner-child doll or imagined). Feel their smallness. Their vulnerability. Their aliveness. You do not need to fix, teach, or stimulate. Your presence is enough.

Silently communicate through gentle sensation:

"I see you."
"I am here."
"You are safe with me."

If it feels right, gently rock the infant or soothingly pet their head and face. Let your calm nervous system guide theirs.

Gaze upon them lovingly and repeat inwardly:

"You are safe with me."
"You don't have to do anything."

"I am not leaving."

Now, allow the roles to gently shift. You are no longer the caregiver. You are the infant.

Feel yourself being held and supported without expectation. Let your body be heavy and your breath slow.

You do not need to respond correctly. You do not need to understand. You are allowed to receive.

Repeat inwardly:

"I am safe right now."
"I am allowed to rest."
"My needs matter."

If emotion arises—tears, resistance, numbness—allow it, knowing your caregiver is there supporting you; their calm presence attuned with your nervous system, showing your body how to regulate challenging experiences with security. Stay with the sensations until your body settles on its own.

Now sense both at once:
The one who holds.
And the one who is held.

Feel safety circulating between them.
Breath softens.
Muscles release.
The body learns through experience.

Rest here for a few moments.

When you're ready, gently bring awareness back to the room—the floor beneath you, the space around you, the present moment.

Before closing, integrate this within your body:

It is safe to be here.
I am supported now.

Remain still for a few breaths allowing integration to continue quietly.

Circuit 1 Integration Questions
Weekly Reflection

- What did I learn about my bio-survival programming this week?
- How has my sense of safety shifted?
- What practices most supported my Circuit 1 activation?
- Where do I still carry survival fear?
- What does my body need to feel safer?
- How is Circuit 1 health affecting my higher circuits?

CHAPTER 4

CIRCUIT 2: BOUNDARIES, EMOTIONS & POWER DYNAMICS

CHAPTER SUMMARY

INDIVIDUALIZATION & SELF-DEFINITION

Following the development of Circuit 1 in early childhood, the young human starts becoming conscious of their own existence as a separate entity from their primary nurturing figure and the environment with which they interact. Now they are able to form concepts of what makes them up, what is theirs, and boundaries with what is not—in short, the personal ego develops. With this separateness comes complex emotional reactions which they understand are their own, and come from within rather than outside.

Primary life directives tend to come from the "four Fs": feeding, fighting, fleeing, and fornication. The fight-or-flight response is an activation of the sympathetic nervous system, which shunts blood to the extremities to allow for a quick physical response to threats and other stressors. Other means of activating the peripheral nervous system and the muscles of the extremities (e.g., intense exercise) are important within the second circuit.

EGO DEVELOPMENT

Imprinting for Circuit 2 generally happens before the age of three, and falls into Piaget's "preoperational" stage of development. The actual formation of the ego—this "separateness"—can prematurely begin before this. Studies of prenatal development have pointed to a direct connection between traumatic events to either the child or mother causing a chemical or hormonal disruption to the womb. The more frequent these traumas, the greater likelihood there is of the child developing a premature sense of self-hood. This early sense of separation from the oceanic oneness of the womb experience can be detrimental to complete and healthy C-1 development, causing stunted neurodevelopment or a negative imprint.

Once the child comes to realize they exist as a sovereign entity, they begin to see the world around them differently—evaluating how to navigate and manipulate their environment and those within it. As this realization sets in, they learn to leverage this to their advantage by manipulating those in the position to meet survival or emotional demands—emotional outbursts, or "tantrums" may be tools used to reach these goals.

Developmentalists consider this a time of pain and selfishness involving high anxiety, paranoia, and egocentrism. Other associations include self-centered power struggles, aggression, hedonism, amorality, and little-to-no impulse control. During this time of development, one learns to take ownership and control of bodily functions including toilet training and mastering gravity through the act of walking. These are key vulnerable points where heavy conditioning and imprinting may occur.

IMPRINTING HIERARCHY

The second circuit imprint defines the sense of personal emotional freedom, family or social hierarchical status, and emotional intelligence. These then form personal values, beliefs, and convictions which can become self-defining factors throughout life.

The child is likely to imprint a tendency toward either an assertive/dominant or a passive/submissive role. A child who takes on a dominant imprint tends to express an "authority reflex": they swell up their muscles and vocalize (yell, growl, howl, etc.) when faced with conflicts and challenges. On the other hand, those who imprint as primarily passive tend to shrink their muscles, lower their head, and slump away from confrontation. (This can also be seen in the behavior of other mammals.)

The emotional-territorial circuit relates to breaking away from the primary nurturing figure and becoming more influenced by the relationship with the disciplinary figure in your life. This is often the paternal figure in the traditional nuclear family, if one is present. This person may be perceived as the child's invincible protector and image of unwavering strength. If this figure has a strong second circuit imprint themselves, and encourages the child to interact with, claim, and have dominion over their space for themselves, the child is likely to also develop a heavily dominant imprint. If this figure has an excessively dominating presence, however, the opposite can happen, creating a passive/submissive imprint as the child is hindered in their attempts at having agency over themselves or their environment.

People develop a particularly strong imprint in situations where there is a greater demand to take control of their environment because of threats (real or perceived), dangers to Self, or a need to protect others. Those who are taught to "listen and not speak" (e.g., internalizing sayings such as "children should be seen and not heard" from adult figures) tend to take a more passive/submissive imprint.

Awareness of Mortality

At this stage the child develops a simplistic perception of their own mortality. Suddenly there is an understanding of a starting point to life, and with that, an understanding there must also be an end.

CRUDE LANGUAGE

Language is still undeveloped during this time period; body language and simplistic vocalizations are the primary means of communication. Simple growls and grunts (or submissive groans or whines), much like other mammals, may be used depending on the imprint. Language may also emphasize violence or bodily functions brought under control during Circuit 2 development; e.g., insults focused around the genitals, feces, or lewd sexual acts. Those with heavy Circuit 2 imprints may favor these into adulthood.

A substantial adult population demonstrates heavy Circuit 2 intelligence, which can be highly adaptive for survival in hostile environments such as inner-city neighborhoods, combat zones, and prisons. However, they may prove problematic in other environments, like office jobs.

TERRITORIALITY

Boundaries and belongings are of key importance to this circuit. The child defines their space or claims things as their own. To stake this claim, the young child may lick or mark an object. Later in life, this plays out as power politics such as exchanges between parent and child, employer and employee, and leaders and followers. Patriotism and nationalism tend to be born from this same drive. Pride in what is "theirs" and where they belong may be a particularly prominent facet of one's personality in those strongly imprinted in this circuit.

Strong emotions may arise if there is a questioning of the sense of Self or territory. The most common reaction is anger. Despite a general cultural stigmatization against expressing anger, it plays an essential function when growth or change becomes stifled, or when one must muster the force to get out of a detrimental situation. Anger may also arise when a drive to move or express oneself is stifled. Boredom also seems an expression of C-2 stagnation where frustration comes out of an internal drive or need for self-challenge, risk-taking, or achievement that is not being met.

"FLEXING"

Participating in events that activate any of these emotional reactions, drives, or opportunities to "flex one's muscles" may appeal to those with strong C-2 imprints. These may be direct challenges or emotional engagement in more dramatic elements of life. Examples of this might be watching the emotional rollercoasters of soap operas; or highly competitive or violent sports including mixed martial arts; or the hybrid of these two examples in the industry of scripted professional wrestling. Making your presence known by making loud sounds to draw attention (including cars, firearms, fireworks, etc.), breaking things (e.g., rage rooms), arm wrestling, chopping wood, and loud music/concerts and associated activities (e.g., mosh pits) are a few other examples.

"YOU'RE EITHER WITH ME OR AGAINST ME"

Thoughts and communications within this circuit typically remain egocentric, with the assumption that others see, hear, and feel exactly as you do. As such, there cannot really be such a thing as a true two-way interpersonal relationship in second-circuit consciousness. Everyone is either "with you or against you." Thoughts remain binary in terms of either being strong/dominant ("haves") or weak/submissive ("have-nots").

THE EMOTIONAL TANK

Acting on drives to satisfy your desires, knowing and acknowledging what you want, and expressing these things maintains a balanced "emotional tank." When your emotional tank becomes depleted—meaning emotions are deficient, not active, or suppressed—it can lead to apathy, depression, and pessimism.

The need to have a sense of control over your life and emotions often lies at the root of this. Too often it can seem as though these negative things are occurring *to* you from external forces rather than from *within*. It can feel like you've lost all ability to control how you react to them. Unfortunately, desperate attempts to feel a degree of control within your life may turn into acts of controlling others. These attempts at control can act as the origins of abuse in work or social environments, or in relationships or domestic violence situations.

PERSONAL POWER

The sense of personal agency and dominion over Self is a major focal point of this circuit. It can be generated through "following your heart." When this is lacking, a victim mentality or paranoia can develop where the world is perceived to be working against you.

The ability to "win" or to feel special supports self-esteem. Goal-setting and the achievement of these goals help to support self-dominion.

NEUROBIOLOGY

Between 10 months to two years of age, there is slow brain growth while the child practices, improves, and perfects already learned skills. As control of movement improves, there is neural pruning (i.e., elimination of weak or unused neural connections) leading to the sharpening of networks for efficiency. If you do not have enough experience, or if your ability to explore the range of possible movements is limited, these networks may not develop to their full potential.

The next major period of brain growth happens between 2–4 years, mostly affecting maturation of the senses. Most children capable of all senses tend to have the same capability to experience sensory input. The child has reached the age of fusion of thought and language development: they may now speak in concepts and think in words. Stunted development may happen if there is a lack of integration or associative learning of this input.

CHAPTER LESSONS

- Emotional expression
- Boundaries/territories
- Power/hierarchical interdynamics
- Ego establishment and maintenance: selfishness
- Saying "no"
- Peripheral nervous system (PNS)—activation and "flexing" of skeletal muscles
- Top dog vs. bottom dog: docility vs. domination
- Leading vs. commanding
- Primality/sexuality/grunting
- Limbic hijacking

GOALS

- Explore how early life circumstances surrounding personal autonomy and interpersonal power dynamics may continue to play out in your daily life as well as your perception/interpretation of reality
- Reflect on how often you operate primarily from Circuit 2 intelligence
- Recognize potential personal C-2 disharmonies or imbalances
- Explore multiple facets of Circuit 2 consciousness
- Consider ways that can work to improve or maximize your Circuit 2 intelligence

QUALITIES OF CIRCUIT 2 DYNAMICS

BALANCED CIRCUIT 2 ENERGY

- Ability to fully accept & experience your feelings
- Ability to form relationships free of emotional neediness/sexual enmeshment
- Friendly, optimistic; concerned for others; has a sense of belonging
- Creative, imaginative, intuitive
- Confident or bold sense of humor

- Empathetic: can merge with the body/mind of another person to better understand them
- Sexual: sensual, radiating a full & healthy sense of sexuality, the highest goal of which is a wonderful orgasm and emotional connection with your partner. Possible desire to have children (healthy reproductive drive)

Excessive Circuit 2 Energy

- Emotionally aggressive, explosive
- Overly ambitious
- Manipulative or controlling
- Caught up in delusion
- Over-indulgent, self-serving, egocentric, proud
- Blunted empathy: unable to distinguish between Self and other; little-to-no awareness or concern for the experiences of others
- Tendency to be prejudiced, manipulative, self-serving
- Sexual: possibly obsessed with thoughts of sex; sees others who are sexually attractive exclusively as sex objects; requires frequent gratification

Deficient Circuit 2 Energy

- Uncontrolled empathy: sensitive to the needs and feelings of others at the expense of Self; poor boundaries
- Inability to differentiate feelings from those of others
- Lack of self-worth, self-negating, resentful
- Inner emptiness leading to unhealthy/codependent relationships
- Martyr complex; distrustful
- Extremely shy, timid, docile; buries emotions
- Attachment, insecurity, frustration
- Burdened by guilt
- Unconscious sexual repression which leads to overwhelming or disturbing sexual dreams; sexual impotence or underactive sexual drive

REFLECTIONS

Core theme: Power, boundaries, attachment, ego development, sense of self

Imprint age: ~2–4 years old

Mantra: *"The sovereign and empowered individual within me recognizes and respects the sovereign and empowered individual within you." "No."*

- **Word Association:** list one or more words that define, or come to mind with, the following emotions:

Anger ______________________________

Rage ______________________________

Anxiety ______________________________

Overwhelmed ______________________________

Dread ______________________________

Vulnerability ______________________________

Admiration ______________________________

Jealousy ______________________________

Resentment ______________________________

Regret ______________________________

Resignation ______________________________

Grief ______________________________

Despair ______________________________

Disgust ______________________________

Pity ______________________________

Empathy ______________________________

Shame ______________________________

Guilt ______________________________

Self-Compassion ______________________________

Connection ______________________________

Love ______________________________

Joy ______________________________

Trust ______________________________

Betrayal ______________________________

Gratitude ______________________________

Relief ______________________________

Pride ______________________________

Humility ______________________________

Tranquility ______________________________

Reflect on a time you were "hijacked" by your emotions

____

____

____

____

____

____

Reflect on a part or role in your life, or a time you were at the "top of the social food chain"

____

____

____

____

____

____

Reflect on a part or role in your life or a time you were in a more subordinate position or at the "bottom of the social food chain"

____

____

____

____

____

____

Reflect on how the two previous situations made you feel. What's the difference? Which feels most familiar/comfortable? Which do you prefer? Why?

____

____

____

____

____

____

How might your early family or social dynamic have influenced how you navigate social situations with respect to hierarchy?

____

____

____

____

____

____

Reflect on your ability to establish and/or maintain personal boundaries. Is this difficult or easy for you?

____

____

____

____

How much of your ego identity is rooted in pride for your region/town/city/state/country?

Do you have a favorite sports team? Why do you support them over others? Is it their success rate? Is it because they are from the same geographic region as you? Is it because your family or a loved one supported them? Is it because you grew up supporting them?

How hard is it for you to tell someone "no"?

How well do you self-regulate your emotions?

What is your biggest/go-to "flex"? Physically? Emotionally? Intellectually? Socially?

What do you do to "get your blood pumping" physically or emotionally?

Do you enjoy physical, adrenaline-inducing thrills such as roller coasters, skydiving, or driving fast? Do you consider yourself an adrenaline junkie?

What makes you feel at your most "primal"?

How does reading and working through this material feel to you? Does it bring up any particular emotions?

Try to identify people (real or fictional) who embody quintessential C-2 characteristics. What are their strengths and flaws?

What would the world look like if Circuit 2 were the primary circuit people operated from?

ACTION STEPS

Activities that activate the peripheral nervous system/skeletal muscles, sympathetic nervous system, and adrenals

ACTIVITIES TO BALANCE C-2

- High impact physical activity: hitting, kicking, push-ups, pushing, pulling, or rocking
- Singing, rapping
- Dancing
- Shouting/screaming into a cushion; crashing into pillows or a crash pad
- Wheelbarrow walking
- Squeezing a stress ball or making playdough; bouncing a ball
- Ripping up or crumpling a piece of paper
- Chewing crunchy foods
- Outdoor activities: raking, sweeping, chopping wood, etc.
- Playing with children, especially in groups; observing hierarchy/power dynamics
- Learning to be in assertive/dominant and/or docile/submissive roles
- Admit to being wrong, even if you are not
- If you are accustomed to losing, create three small victories
- Watch sophomoric/slapstick comedy
- Uphold your integrity/accountability
- C-2 yoga/Reichian pelvic exercises
- Get your adrenaline going; hype yourself up

REPAIRING EARLY CIRCUIT 2 WOUNDS

Notice how you relate to assertion and restraint in your daily life. When you want something, are you able to move toward it with ease, or do you waver or justify/over-explain? When you need to say no, does your body tense up or shut down in discomfort? Instead of saying no, do you find yourself people-pleasing, apologizing, or sacrificing your own needs for others? Circuit 2 wounds resulting in deficiency often show up as self-doubt about personal power: feeling responsible for others, equating assertiveness with conflict, vacillating between compliance and defensiveness, submission to others.

Rather than trying to correct these patterns, begin by noticing them as signals. Ask yourself:

What does my "no" need in order to feel safe?
What does my "yes" need in order to feel grounded?
Where do I shrink, and where do I push, instead of simply standing my ground?

Or, conversely, notice how you relate to control, influence, and emotional intensity. Do you indulge in the power of asserting "yes" and "no" at the expense of others, justifying yourself as entitled, disregarding other's rights/needs/feelings, or desiring to exert control/influence? Circuit 2 wounds resulting in *excess* C-2 energy can show up as dominance, emotional force, impatience with vulnerability or uncertainty, or discomfort when not in control.

Rather than suppressing this energy, first notice it and ask yourself:

What happens in my body when I don't assert immediately?
Can I remain present without influencing the outcome?
What do I fear would happen if I didn't take control?

Healthy Circuit 2 functioning is about feeling self-assured and confident to occupy your place clearly, calmly, and without justification. Integration happens when your body learns that separation does not threaten connection, boundaries do not require aggression, and emotional intensity can be felt without being acted out. When your focus shifts from the extreme polarities of power vs. self-doubt, you become emotionally available and present for authentic connection, autonomy, and choice. Allow this understanding to become behavior through small, ordinary moments of self-awareness and intentional practice.

POWER MAPPING

Objective: Understand your current relationship with power

CREATE A POWER MAP

Draw a circle representing yourself in the center of a page. Around the circle, map all significant relationships and institutions, sizing and positioning them based on:

- Size = the amount of power they hold in your life
- Distance = the emotional/psychological proximity
- Color = the feeling tone (e.g., red=conflict, green=harmonious, yellow=neutral)

Include: family, boss, colleagues, friends, government, religion, inner critic, etc.

ANALYSIS

- Who/what holds disproportionate power over you?
- Where do you give your power away?
- Where do you claim appropriate power?
- Where do you dominate inappropriately?
- What patterns do you notice?

Action: Choose one relationship where you'll reclaim or rebalance power this month.

THE ANGER/AGGRESSION INQUIRY

Purpose: Develop healthy relationship with anger

REFLECTIVE WRITING

Your Anger History

* How was anger expressed in your family of origin?
* What happened when you got angry as a child?

* What messages did you receive about anger?
* How do you express (or suppress) anger now?

Current Anger Inventory

* What am I currently angry about? (List everything, big and small)
* What is the anger protecting or pointing to?
* What boundary has been violated?
* What needs to change?

Anger Expression Styles

Mark where you fall on each spectrum. (You may have multiple marks on each spectrum.) Reflect on how your expression might change based on context and triggers:

Suppressed	|-------|-------|-------|	Explosive
Passive	|-------|-------|-------|	Aggressive
Indirect	|-------|-------|-------|	Direct

Goal: Move toward direct, bound, appropriate anger expression

Posture & Body Language Awareness

Notice how you walk, stand, and occupy space when you enter an occupied room. What does your body language say to others? Experiment with widening vs. narrowing your stance, moving with intention, standing straight and tall, maintaining good eye contact when speaking, and practicing other postures and gestures that imply confidence. This is not about dominating or intimidating others, but to embody a confident presence.

Safe Expression of Aggression

Notice where you store aggression and tension in your body. Choose an appropriate physical expression to release it from those places as Circuit 2 needs discharge to regulate. For example, if you feel like your voice is weak or oppressed, sing or scream loudly when you're alone, or yell into a pillow.

Or, if you have been bullied and feel disempowered, imagine yourself as a large ape, grunting and beating your chest in a display of power, strength, and dominance. Notice how it feels when you release pent-up tension, tightness, and stuckness, or shift from disempowered to empowered expressions. Check-in with your body daily and practice some form of safe aggression expression as appropriate.

Circuit 2 Re-Imprinting Meditation: Emerging Self & Healthy Assertion

Begin by finding a comfortable, supported position. Bring your attention to the feeling of being—in your body, in this moment, occupying your own space. Notice your breath as it is; do not adjust it.

Now, gently sense your skin, the outline of your body. Observe the boundary where "you" end, and everything else appears separate from you. Silently acknowledge, "I am separate, yet I am safe."

Bring your attention to the space around your body. Notice how you can be aware of the world without needing to merge with it or push it away.

Allow yourself to feel confident occupying that space, neither inflated nor withdrawn, but fully present.

Now reflect on the act of saying "no," neither defensively nor defiantly, but firmly and assertively. Observe how your body responds to setting the boundary of "no." Notice any tension, relief, reluctance, or steadiness.

Silently repeat, *"I am allowed to say no. I do not have to disappear to belong."*

Now imagine the act of saying "yes." Yes to curiosity, exploration, and moving toward what interests and pleases you.

Compare the feelings of saying "yes" vs. saying "no."

Now bring your attention to your sacral chakra (just below your belly), a place of emotional power.

Imagine this center as steady and responsive:

Able to feel emotion without overwhelm.

Able to assert without dominating.
Able to belong without self-negating.

Acknowledge to yourself:

My feelings matter.
I can regulate and respond.

Lean into this affirmation for a few breaths.

As you prepare to return, bring your attention back to your skin, your boundary with the world. Feel this boundary as solid, yet flexible.

Internalize that you are not required to prove your place to anyone. You have the power to be just as you are and to move freely of your own will.

When you're ready, gently return to ordinary awareness.

Circuit 2 Integration Questions
Weekly Reflection

- What did I learn about my emotional-territorial programming this week?
- How has my sense of power, confidence, or self-protection shifted?
- What practices most supported my Circuit 2 activation?
- Where do I still freeze, submit, attack, or overcompensate?
- What does my body need to feel strong, defended, and capable?
- How is Circuit 2 health affecting my higher circuits?

CHAPTER 5

CIRCUIT 3: MAP-MAKING, LOGIC & PROBLEM-SOLVING

CHAPTER SUMMARY

Around the age of seven or eight years old, children tend to transition into another phase of life. Until this point, their experience of the world was from the realm of imaginative and superstitious thinking. As the frontal lobes of the brain develop further, they begin to apply logic and rational thinking about the physical world. In developmental psychology, this falls into what has been called the "concrete operational stage."

SEPARATING EXPERIENCE FROM IMAGINATION

A major part of this stage is the ability to intellectually separate hard interpretations of experiences from metaphoric information and symbolic representations of reality. Prior to this skill, stories, fairy tales, television shows, movies, or imagined situations would be no less real (with no less impact on the psyche and nervous system) than direct, lived experience. Superstitious and fantastical thinking were taken literally, and the nervous system registered it with the same intensity as any other event. For example, a scary movie is experienced in nearly the same way as a frightening or traumatic real-life event, but with C-3 development, the child becomes able to recognize that this is not a legitimate threat. Improved cognitive abilities let thinking override physiological activation.

Symbolic Intelligence

Symbols and abstract language become available. With this comes writing and recording which allow for the passing on of meaning and information beyond oral communication, and for a more concrete conceptualization of the linear passage of time. Information can be spread over and through time. We become bound in time.

Categorization, Organization, & Compartmentalization

With the development of the third circuit comes the ability to mentally organize and categorize objects and events. The ability to create associations among multiple sources of information, and compare and contrast incoming information, makes it easier to commit to memory. An internal dialog begins to form for many people (interestingly, some people never develop this internal monologue). Thought experiments and philosophical considerations become more available. These abilities are largely responsible for much of the historical innovation and acceleration of logic, science, technology, and the availability of information.

Emotional Hijacking

The third circuit can be easily overtaken by the first two circuits. If information activates these lower circuits with either survival anxiety or emotional engagement, these will tend to override logic altogether. This has been referred to as "limbic hijacking." Survival and emotions take precedence in most cases, and will demand to be taken care of before resuming logical thinking.

Emotional Denial

Individuals with particularly strong third circuit imprints may ignore, or even become hostile toward, the functions of C-1 and C-2 that have not served them well. The drives of these circuits may be seen as illogical or puzzling as they do not adhere to rational logic. Anything involving playfulness or doing something "just for fun" can be dismissed as ridiculous, silly, or childish.

HAND-EYE-VOICE-BRAIN COORDINATION

Third circuit imprints have associations with the delicate muscles of the larynx and the fine motor movements of the hands, which allows for verbal diversity and increased dexterity and tool use. Eighty percent of people exhibit subtle motor movements of the mouth, jaw, tongue, and vocal chords when thinking or reading; this is called subvocalization (silent speech). These traits are found in higher mammals and seem most developed in humans and cetaceans such as whales and dolphins.

RIGIDITY IN THOUGHT

Those who have a strong third circuit and come to recognize how its model-building actually works to define one's reality become able to redefine their reality on their own symbolic and linguistic terms. This is explored further in Chapter 10 regarding Circuit 7. The language, metaphors, and definitions people use strongly influence how they think, influencing not only the words used, but *how* they are used and culturally defined. To redefine terms is to redefine perception.

Confusion or dissonance results when ideas, concepts, and thought patterns do not coincide with your true symbolic nature. When you are unable to differentiate incoming information from internal biases of "who you are" by self-definition or models already in place, mental clarity suffers. When this is the case, you can have a false sense of objectivity, often with an inability to update models as new information comes in.

INFORMATION ACCUMULATION & NEGATIVE ENTROPY

The rate at which information is processed and communication happens in the third circuit can become overwhelming, wherein logic and thinking can become rapid-fire. When the semantic circuit is too active, it may seem as though the mind is always turned on—talking rapidly about ideas, concepts, and facts from a scientific, analytical, or "objective" perspective.

This circuit—and particularly, the information gathered within this circuit—has a negatively entropic nature, meaning that information tends to accumulate and create greater and greater degrees of order rather than break down into chaos. Technology, curiosity, philosophy, and information-gathering continues to grow exponentially over time. As we will see in the next chapter, evolution and society have a built-in brake for this runaway logic train with Circuit 4.

NEUROBIOLOGY

Around 4–5 years of age, synthesis of new brain cells comes to a virtual halt. Despite this, the brain increases about 30% in weight after that age due to increased neural connectivity throughout the brain, allowing for more complex mental functioning. Around age six, connections are driven by the thalamus, and form between previously separate mental and sensorimotor functions, resulting in concrete reasoning. Between the ages of eight and 10, significant changes in myelination and cell body size in the prefrontal cortex occur. Around age 10, the next rapid brain growth stage begins with significant neural pruning, connecting earlier-organized networks and their derivative mental functions behind concrete reasoning.

CHAPTER LESSONS

- Logic, reason, science, concrete operations
- Problem-solving
- Deconstructing and compartmentalizing ideas
- Rational intelligence
- Exponential growth of technology
- Doing more with less (ephemeralization)
- Language/laryngeal vibrations
- Dexterity, fine finger-movements

- Linear causality
- Symbolic interpretation and use
- C-3 without an evolutionary break would go on *ad infinitum*

GOALS

- Consider/explore how often you primarily use or rely on linear/logical rationale in your daily life/decision-making
- Consider any influences in later childhood that may have influenced how much or how little you utilize logic
- Recognize potential personal C-3 imbalances and disharmonies
- Explore multiple facets of C-3 intelligence
- Consider ways that you may work to maximize, improve, or balance your C-3 intelligence

QUALITIES OF CIRCUIT 3 DYNAMICS

BALANCED CIRCUIT 3 ENERGY

- Cheerful and respectful toward Self and others
- Strong sense of personal power; abundant physical energy
- Emotional stability; strong metabolism, digestion and constitution
- Dynamism, perseverance, achievement
- Skillful, intelligent, relaxed, spontaneous; takes on new challenges and ideas
- Enjoys puzzles and problem-solving
- Enjoys physical activity and good food
- Sexual: cares about one's partner; sense of responsibility toward mate and children; uninhibited and relaxed; can show warmth

EXCESSIVE CIRCUIT 3 ENERGY

- Overly intellectual and judgmental; workaholic, perfectionist
- Jealous, judgmental, critical, condescending
- May use drugs to relax

- As employer: demanding; as employee: resents authority
- Superficial superiority complex with hidden inferiority complex
- Prone to nausea, vomiting; easily startled; hyperactivity to sound
- Sexual: demanding, tests one's partner; complains about relationship a lot; rarely fulfilled, sexually aloof; may not find sex logical or a worthwhile pursuit

DEFICIENT CIRCUIT 3 ENERGY

- Depressed, low energy; apathy, hyperemotionality
- Confused
- Lacks confidence/motivation; inability to follow through
- Worries about what others will think; feels controlled by others
- Poor digestion and overall health
- Afraid of being alone
- General intolerance to too much information/stimuli
- Sexual: insecure, in need of constant reassurance; jealous, lack of trust

REFLECTIONS

Core theme: Language/symbolic thought and representation, meaning-making, abstract thinking

Imprint age: ~7 years old

Mantra: *"The map is not the territory"* (Korzybski). *"Thoughts are tools, not rulers and I can re-narrate my story." "I am not required to believe everything I think."*

How easily do you learn/process math? Reading? Writing? Science?

How often do you make lists/spreadsheets? Do you only make necessary to-do lists, or do you use lists/spreadsheets for seemingly everything?

Relative to C-1/C-2 development—have you ever felt you shut off your emotions/body, opting instead for logic?

How many languages do you speak? How easily do you learn a new one?

How often do you feel "stuck in your head"?

How often do you feel like you are ruminating or have cyclical thoughts?

Explain how you feel and what your thought processes are like when highly caffeinated.

Do you enjoy trying to figure out how something works?

What is a topic you could talk about at length or give a lecture on?

Do you feel you have good or poor hand-eye coordination?

Do you have an internal monologue/dialogue when you think? Does this have a particular voice? Your own or others?

At what age did you learn to read? Do you remember if this was easy or difficult? How much do you read now? What kind of material do you enjoy reading? What did you enjoy reading as a kid?

If you could solve one problem to improve your life, what would it be? List at least 3 steps toward achieving this.

How easily do you get distracted? How easily do you multitask?

Do you have a favorite quote? Why is it your favorite?

What is the point of reading and working through this material?

Try to identify people (real or fictional) who embody quintessential C-3 characteristics. What are their strengths and flaws?

What would the world look like if Circuit 3 was the primary circuit people operated from?

ACTION STEPS

Activities that activate higher order cognitive functions will work the third circuit. Some examples include:

- Making lists, schematics, charts, spreadsheets, diagrams, models, or maps
- Studying/research; particularly logical topics such as the sciences or mathematics
- Writing/storytelling: poems, fables, proverbs, jokes, essays, books
- Word games and trivia questions
- Philosophizing—preferably involving as many people with differing viewpoints as possible
- Problem-solving and challenging oneself by breaking patterns and finding a solution
- Puzzle/problem-solving; video games—also integrates hand-eye coordination
- Hand-eye activities to get out of your head (knitting, crochet, video games, pottery, sculpting, coloring, fidget toys/tools)
- Counting/organizing things
- Taking something seemingly metaphysical/irrational and attempting to create a rational explanation
- Listing the morning/evening routine
- Writing a philosophy/research paper
- Draw a schematic of the linear developmental progression of Circuits 1–3
- Programming (computer, audio, etc.), engineering, accounting

YOUR MENTAL FILING SYSTEM

Sketch how you store information: A library? A maze? a chaotic junk drawer? What needs re-shelving or re-organizing?

MINDFUL META-COGNITION EXERCISE

Set a timer for 5 minutes and label thoughts as they arise as "remembering," "judging," "perceiving," "planning," etc. This shifts you into the position of an observer. Practice this randomly throughout the day.

Symbolic Play: Draw or diagram a problem using shapes, lines, or scribbles instead of words. This can help to loosen semantic rigidity.

CIRCUIT 3 RE-IMPRINTING MEDITATION: TIME-BINDING RELEASE

Find a comfortable position sitting upright but relaxed and supported. Take one slow breath in through the nose...and a long exhale through the mouth.

Again—inhale, receiving peace... Exhale, releasing, surrender...

Now bring your attention to your mind. Not thoughts themselves (yet), but the *activity* of naming, labeling, interpreting.

Notice how quickly the mind explains experience.

You don't need to stop this. Just observe it.

Silently say:

"This is the circuit of meaning."

Now see if you can locate the "narrative center." Bring awareness to the area around the throat, jaw, tongue, and temples. This is where language often lives in the body.

If there's tension, let it be there. If there's movement, let it move. Just noticing...

Now think of a familiar phrase or belief that tends to run automatically—something that influences your experience of self and reality. Condense it to a single phrase.

Hold it lightly, delibly, as if written in pencil. On the next exhale, repeat the phrase and allow it to gently loosen and dissolve. Then pause, and silently say:

"This is a description, not reality."

Now allow a new sentence to form—not an affirmation, not a correction. Something simple and accurate. Examples (choose one or let your own arise):

"I am allowed to revise meaning."
"Beliefs and understanding can change."
"Words serve me; I don't serve words."

Repeat it and feel how the body responds to this repatterning, just noticing how it feels. Imagine old phrases, inherited beliefs, outdated conclusions—like files being archived to a shelf labeled *"No longer current."*

Silently say:

"Thank you. You can rest now."

Notice any softening in the face, throat, or chest. Bring attention back to the breath as you integrate this experience. Before opening your eyes, silently acknowledge:

"Meaning is flexible."

When you're ready, gently return—bringing with you a little more spaciousness around thought. Practice this time-binding release with other beliefs and mental patterns.

CIRCUIT 3 INTEGRATION QUESTIONS WEEKLY REFLECTION

- What did I learn about my cognitive programming this week?
- How has my relationship with language, logic, and meaning-making shifted?
- What practices most supported my Circuit 3 activation?

- Where do I still get trapped in mental loops, overthinking, or rigid maps?
- What does my nervous system need to think clearly without tightening or dissociating?
- How is Circuit 3 health affecting my higher circuits?

CHAPTER 6

CIRCUIT 4: SEXUALITY, COMMUNITY & MORALITY

CHAPTER SUMMARY

The socio-sexual circuit develops and initially imprints around the time of adolescence, and slows down the negatively entropic nature of Circuit 3. Where curiosity, discovery, and scientific innovation progresses at an exponential rate with the third circuit, the fourth circuit turns your focus to interpersonal relationships and social interactions. Peer groups, along with emotional and sexual attractions, tend to become a primary focus.

SOCIAL DYNAMICS

This circuit is defined by the ability to relate to others. When the foundations of the first three circuits have been established (i.e., safety [C-1], emotionality and sense of Self [C-2], and model-building to comprehend the world [C-3]), the next natural step becomes extending beyond Self to sharing and interacting with others (C-4). There is also a strong urge to seek a feeling of belonging to something "bigger than yourself."

While you choose the type of group or social dynamic that best suits you, previous life experiences may influence the direction you move toward. This both further validates these prior life experiences and allows you to learn from shared experiences and the reality tunnels of others.

Many developmental models of psychology describe up through this stage in various ways and go no further (i.e., psychospiritual and other transpersonal states that have come to be considered "non-ordinary" with respect to these primary normative stages of development). This is likely due to the fact that nearly all models maintain that the majority of adults operate at or below this level most of the time. As such, the first four circuits may be considered the mainstream consciousness within most "Westernized" modern cultures.

Sub-Phases from Adolescence to Adulthood to the Collective

Antero Alli notes three sub-phases that an individual goes through: adolescence (aka the "big kid" stage); the "adulthood" stage; and the collectivization stage.

Adolescence, AKA the "Big Kid" Stage

This stage is primarily characterized by self-indulgence, egotism, and narcissism. Motives and goals are mostly self-based, and often result in actions considered "socially irresponsible." This acts to establish personal independence—transitioning from a state of dependence on caregivers to one of relative independence. This stage entails a high degree of what may be considered "social immaturity." Recent evidence shows that contemporary youth has an extended period of immaturity compared to prior generations in the form of "play" and schooling. This longer "play" period may be the result of the increasing complexity of our world and its technologies. This complexity demands the development of more intricate and exhaustive skill sets. It has been argued that this may also serve the adaptive purpose of extending the period of brain plasticity. That is, the more complex technology and society becomes, a longer period of "playfulness" or "immaturity" is required to prolong proliferation of new neural connections to keep up and adapt.

THE "ADULTHOOD" STAGE

This stage involves the setting of social responsibilities, maintenance of a regular schedule or routine, and an emphasis on keeping events organized according to linear time and cultural expectations. This includes moving into a parental and family role. This is also the stage in which many become socially "domesticated" as their previously irresponsible behavior becomes more tame and regimented in accordance with cultural expectations.

COLLECTIVIZATION STAGE

Here you seek out and identify with something larger than the Self and larger than the family dynamic of the adulthood stage. Often this involves joining groups or extended "families" that have their own moral codes and social rules. These groups may be as diverse as churches, military or veterans' groups, communes, gangs, support groups, or subcultures/gatherings depending on what you identify with. Belonging to a particular group, may involve sacrificing individual differences and your sense of "right and wrong" for the sake of the socially defined moral code. It has been called "conformist consciousness," with the choice of actions being labelled "institutional," "conventional," or "traditional." All of these express the compulsion for an externally established organization or peer group to act as a moral guidepost of choices. With this, you may also develop a prejudice or fear toward those outside the group, which can result in projected anger or even hatred towards outsiders in an "us versus them" dichotomy. You may also develop a preoccupation with meeting expectations of appearance, preferences, and behavior.

EXPANDED PERSPECTIVE & AWARENESS OF SELF

Out of the collective stage, and within the confines of the social setting, the first signs of true personal authority begin to develop. At the same time, an objective empathy emerges as the world becomes increasingly viewed beyond the solely individual perspective. Many more points of view are now considered, all of which hold some sense of validity. This allows you to step beyond personal experience and see things independently from the original experiences that formed the viewpoint. You become able to observe your perspective without being fully immersed in it.

EXTERNAL VALIDATION, CONFORMITY, & GUILT

Feelings of guilt and shame also become prominent components at this stage due to the heavy focus on external validation, acceptance, and conforming to a group expectation or moral set. People spend a great deal of time hiding their true selves by projecting a socially expected and accepted one. You may begin doing things because you "should" rather than what you want or what you feel is the "right" thing to do. This may become justified under "everyone else is doing it"; or you may fear the judgment of others if you do not adhere to collective expectations. This is the world of peer and social pressure. Guilt and shame become means of maintaining duties and obligation to groups of authority figures while maintaining the status quo and deterring non-conformity. Your sense of right may become defined by what ultimately contributes to the group and sustains the social order.

TYPES OF GUILT

Animal Guilt: when there is a direct, intuitive sense that doing something is "wrong" *before* performing the action. This is your knowledge of right and wrong—the internal moral compass.

Conditioned Guilt: generally felt *after* doing something you have learned to be morally "wrong," and after it has been mentally processed and triggers a reaction to a particular moral program. This can build resentment over these feelings. This type of guilt becomes a major factor of the fourth circuit. If the guilt is unjustified or seems to happen for no apparent reason, it may develop into feelings of self-consciousness, embarrassment, or social ineptitude. If this continues, passive-aggressive or unconscious manipulative behavior can become commonplace.

Reproductive Drive & Sexual Imprints

This circuit becomes activated and imprinted around puberty as the genetic code awakens hormonal shifts and matures the organs of sexual reproduction. The imprints tend to be acute: the first sexual symbols or experiences often define what is sexually arousing throughout life. While any sex role is possible prior to imprinting, once imprinting happens, a particular sex role can become solidified. This includes matters of sexual preference including physical features like hair or eye color, body shapes, etc. This imprint, if negative, may result in sexual dysfunctions or unpleasurable attitudes toward sexuality. Sex aversion or repulsion are examples.

Rites of Passage & Coming of Age Imprinting

Many cultures recognize how positive or negative experiences can influence nervous system development that could impact lifelong tendencies; thus, initiations ("rites of passage") during this critical time of imprint vulnerability have been used to imprint culturally desired traits. Passage into adolescence or adulthood (and, thus, into the adult role within society) seems most widespread, although many cultures also do this during other imprint periods.

Rule Learning

At the conformist level of consciousness, many logical inconsistencies exist while conceptual constructs remain limited to absolute and dualistic thinking. The limbic system's influence remains apparent in the inability to tolerate ambiguity. Internal conflicts between cognitive imperatives and emotional reflexes can be frequent: the ongoing tug-of-war between head and heart.

APPEAL TO AUTHORITY

Internal conflicts and a lack of clarity around who you are can lead a to greater compromise of identity to external authority figures and social structures to provide guidance. Others may have a greater ability to manipulate or exploit your sense of Self as it lacks definition. A tendency to appeal to authority figures is generally not beholden to one particular person, but rather a general appeal to the *position of authority* and whoever happens to hold that position. This reliance on external groupthink can be taken to such a degree that someone can belong to multiple groups that hold directly opposing views without it seeming to cause any upset or dissonance to the psyche.

MENTALIZING / THEORY OF MIND

Theory of mind, or mentalizing, refers to the ability to assign mental states—including beliefs, intents, desires, pretending, knowledge, and sarcasm—to yourself and others. This is an understanding that others have beliefs, desires, intentions, and perspectives that may be different than your own.

The mirror neuron system (which learns by observing and copying), responds to the actions, intentions, and emotions of both the Self and others. Over time, a stronger sense of identity and agency forms as interpersonal relations become more stable, and those that prove reliable are more likely to be maintained throughout times of change and life challenges.

FAMILY LIFE—A SOCIETAL BRAKE

Once an adult sex role has been attained, it often includes finding a mate and reproducing. As noted earlier, this often acts as a type of cultural brake for the philosophical musings and curiosities of the third circuit. The cultural demands of a career, the needs of children, etc. can consume much of the time and energy previously available for such ponderings and activities. For this reason, some philosophical or spiritual teachings suggest (or require) a vow of celibacy to deter from this and keep full dedication to the practice or institution.

IMPACTS OF SOCIAL EXCLUSION & REJECTION

Isolation (or social exclusion) can have drastic effects on the psyche and the nervous system. Youths who experience chronic rejection show more activity in the anterior cingulate region of the brain during social inclusion. This brain region has been implicated in the experience of suffering, unfairness, conflict monitoring, expectation violation, and social exclusion in adults. Evidence shows that social deprivation can also have a negative impact on overall lifespan.

NEUROBIOLOGY

Adolescents show a pattern of activation and behavior distinct from both pre-adolescents and adults. Experience-dependent neural plasticity appears to peak in adolescence with gradual but consistent decreases with age. Brain areas implicated in emotional processing, reward processing, and motivation undergo significant change with the reorganization of neural networks that support social behaviors around mate selection and the act of mating.

While many new neural connections happen during this time, significant neural pruning also happens on synapses that are no longer effective or necessary. This frees up metabolic energy which can be devoted to more useful neurons and synapses.

Three core systems become reorganized at puberty:

- Processing basic attention and visual orientation, allowing for better "reading" of faces, emotional expressions, and affect
- "Mentalizing"—the ability to understand the mental state of yourself and others
- Emotion processing

The amygdala also seems to play an important role in shaping adolescent behavior and response to the social world—so much so that it has been called an "agent of change in adolescent neural networks." It helps to strengthen other key brain regions of sociality, and recognizes their positions in response to the dynamic needs of each developmental stage.

There is evidence of disproportionately increased activation of reward systems in adolescent neurodevelopment. When *actual* outcomes do not match an *expected* outcome in an experience, it is processed by what's called "predictive error signaling," which seems to be coded by dopamine cells. This mismatch provides novel information for the person, who then learns something new. Dopamine neurons fire with experiences that include rewards, food or drug consumption, social interactions, and unexpected experiences (surprise!). During adolescence, risky decision-making and behavior creates a sense of reward by increased dopamine. This has been found to be even more so in the presence of peers.

Chapter Lessons

- Social/societal/family roles
- Communities, groups, cultures
- Social expectations
- Conformity
- Bonding and sexuality
- Guilt and shame
- Three sub-phases: adolescence, adulthood, and community

Goals

- Consider/explain how much influence C-4 intelligence plays within your life and how much of your life tends to be driven by C-4 components of sociality

- Consider major events/experiences around the time of puberty/ adolescence that may have had a lasting influence on current life dynamics/decisions
- Recognize/explore potential personal C-4 imbalances/disharmonies
- Explore multiple facets of C-4 intelligence
- Consider ways that may maximize, improve, or balance C-4 intelligence

CHECKLIST OF SOCIETAL MORAL STRUCTURES

- Folkways examples—nose picking, saying please/thank you, respecting elders, sleeping at nighttime, sitting in chairs
- Mores examples—do not steal, no arson, no assaulting peers, no destroying public property, no cheating on tests
- Taboos examples (culturally dependent)—no cannibalism, no necrophilia, no eating the "food of the chief," no killing of sacred animals, no murder, sex is bad/dirty/impure

QUALITIES OF CIRCUIT 4 DYNAMICS

BALANCED CIRCUIT 4 ENERGY

- Friendly, outgoing, able to connect with others
- Compassionate, selfless action, humanitarian
- Creativity, spiritual love, spiritual charity
- Sees the good in everyone, desires to nurture others
- Active in community
- In touch with feelings, empathetic (may feel their aches and pains)
- Discriminating
- Sexual: able to surrender/merge in a love relationship; desires oneness of the body, mind, and soul; strong willpower (can wait for the right partner)

EXCESSIVE CIRCUIT 4 ENERGY

- Demanding, possessive, overly critical

- Moody, melodramatic
- May use money or sex to control people
- Tense between the shoulder blades
- Attitude of a martyr
- Master of conditional love ("I'll love you if...")
- Withholds love to get desired behavior
- Excessive appeal to authority/institution, conformity
- Guilt and shame felt around thoughts and actions that are considered "inappropriate"
- Emphasizes social life or social appearances over personal wellbeing

DEFICIENT CIRCUIT 4 ENERGY

- Feels sorry for yourself
- Inability to love Self which leads to insincerity, codependence
- Insecure, indecisive; may isolate
- Paranoia
- Feels unworthy of love, terrified of rejection, needs reassurance
- Difficulty reaching out/making connection
- Superficial social interactions
- Afraid of letting go, being free, getting hurt, family members getting hurt, abandonment

REFLECTIONS

Core theme: Social identity/role, relationships and intimacy, belonging

Imprint age: Adolescence

Mantras: *"I can belong without losing my individuality." "I can choose which roles I keep." "I am shaped by culture not owned by it." "I am allowed to evolve beyond other people's expectations."*

List and reflect on communities or groups you currently belong to or have belonged to in the past.

____

____

____

____

____

____

What do/did the above groups provide? How did you feel in these groups? Do/did you feel like you belong?

____

____

____

____

____

____

How much of your authentic Self do you feel like you are able to express in the company of other members of these groups?

____

____

____

____

Reflect on your sexual preferences and features you find yourself attracted to. Do you have a "type"? Consider if this has been influenced by an early sexual experience? Early life experiences?

Are there any patterns or tendencies in a social, romantic, or sexual sense that you do not consider ideal or feel would be worth changing?

How was your early adolescence? Overall, was it positive or negative?

Do you find it easy or difficult to connect to others? Immediately or after a while?

List various adult roles you currently occupy (e.g., parent, job, student, mentor, brother/sister, child, etc.). Did you choose these roles intentionally? If not, why/how did you end up in that role (e.g., unplanned pregnancy, parents pressuring a particular career path, etc.)?

What are some taboos you abide by? Are there any that you would find appealing to subvert? How does the thought of breaking these make you feel?

Reflect on any time you broke or transcended existing or previous taboos and how that felt.

What are some roles you no longer hold or may no longer serve you? What roles can you imagine that would serve you better?

What authority figures or institutions do you defer your behavior to? Why?

Who is your "tribe"? How do you interact with those outside of this tribe?

What are qualities you seek out in connecting with others? Have these preferences been influenced by others (e.g., family, religious beliefs or institutions, political ideologies, etc.)?

Try to identify people (real or fictional) who embody quintessential C-4 characteristics. What are their strengths and flaws?

What would the world look like if Circuit 4 was the primary circuit people operated from?

ACTION STEPS

- Hugging a real person or reaching outward as if to connect (you may wish to imagine a friend, partner, family member, or someone in need of support; or meeting someone new, a role model or admired figure; you may also wish to use a stuffed toy or other representative object)
- Making new friends
- Determine qualities and virtues personally desired in friends, confidants, and role models
- Attending social gatherings or group events
- Trying something new
- Breaking previously held taboos

- Couples or group dancing or music-making
- Communal storytelling
- Other communal affairs
- Group/bonding/community-building activities

ROLE EXPERIMENT

Choose one aspect of your persona that you frequently perform and identify with (e.g., helper, expert, rebel, hippie) and intentionally drop it for a day. Do not explain yourself to others. Observe how this change makes you feel and how others react.

EROTIC EXPLORATION

Engage in something sensual (movement, scent, music, touch) with no goal of sexual arousal or release. This retrains eros as life force and presence rather than a goal-oriented performance.

RELATIONAL TRUTH SENTENCE

With a trusted person (or imaginally in writing), consider *"When I am with you, I notice I become_______."*

Repeat this exercise with different people in your life (family, friends, colleagues, acquaintances, strangers you meet). How consistent are you with different people? In what ways do you change or relate differently with various types of people?

CIRCUIT 4 RE-IMPRINTING MEDITATION: BELONGING WITHOUT SELF-ERASURE

Dim the lights and choose a comfortable seated or lying position. Allow your body to settle naturally. There is nothing you need to prepare or achieve.

Begin by gently regulating your breath. Inhale easily. Exhale a little more slowly. Let your nervous system find its own rhythm.

Bring to mind the *social world*—not specific people yet, but the felt sense of being seen, known, evaluated, included or excluded.

Notice what happens in your body. Do not analyze. Simply observe.

Now imagine yourself standing in a shared space—a village, a circle, a room, a community. Others are present, but they are not watching you closely. There is no immediate demand.

Feel your body here.

Notice whether you brace, perform, shrink, adapt, or disappear. Let whatever pattern arises be allowed.

Now gently imagine something new.

You are still seen, but you are not required to shape-shift to remain included.

Feel what it would be like to be recognized without being managed.

Let your posture soften.

Let your breath deepen.

Silently repeat, letting the words land in your body:

> *"I can belong without disappearing."*
> *"I am allowed to be myself here."*

If discomfort arises (e.g., shame, fear, vigilance, grief), allow it to move through at its own pace. You do not need to resolve it.

Now imagine one or two figures in this space who are capable of healthy presence.

Notice how it feels to be met without correction. Without comparison. Without expectation.

Let your body register this as a real experience.

Repeat inwardly:

> *"Connection does not require self-betrayal."*
> *"I do not have to earn belonging."*

Stay here for several breaths.

Feel the difference between being accepted *for your role* vs. being accepted *as you are*.

Let that difference imprint somatically.

When you're ready, gently allow the image to fade. Bring awareness back to the room. Feel the support beneath you.

Before closing, let this integrate:

> *You are allowed to exist in relationship without abandoning yourself.*
> *You belong to yourself first.*

Remain still for a few breaths as you internalize this insight.

Circuit 4 Integration Questions
Weekly Reflection

- What did I learn about my social bonding and role-based programming this week?
- How has my sense of belonging (in relationships, community, or tribe) shifted?
- What practices most supported my Circuit 4 activation?
- Where do I still over-adapt, act from persona, or fear social rejection?
- Which roles or relationships feel nourishing? Which feel constricting or false?
- How is Circuit 4 health affecting my higher circuits?

Chapter 7

Chapel Perilous & Spiritual Emergencies

Chapter Summary

The transition between the fourth circuit and activation of the following transpersonal circuits can be tumultuous. This marks a transition out of well-established societal structures and organization into what appears to be a seemingly chaotic, introspective imperative toward self-driven authenticity. To do this entails a leap in perspective that many don't make. It comes with challenges and impending cultural backlash or scrutiny. For those willing to press forward, there are often instances where the ego-self feels thrown into a whirlwind and displaced, left to wander, trying to find its way back.

Robert Anton Wilson and Antero Alli both called this space "Chapel Perilous." Historically, it has also been called the "dark night of the soul," the alchemical "nigredo," "the abyss," etc.

A Disorienting Existential Limbo

Chapel Perilous is an existential limbo, usually full of confusion and disorientation. As a result, feelings of anxiety, fear, and loneliness often arise. You can find yourself feeling lost and outside of yourself. You can feel out of place, both from society and within, seeming to lack any "home base" to reliably return. You may feel as though you have lost your footing on Self and reality. Life may begin to feel like a movie in which you are in a role merely to be acted out. The world around you may no longer seem to make sense, or may seem to be crumbling into pieces.

The Path Is Not Linear

While the movement between the fourth circuit to the more complex circuits is a common stumbling point, you can enter this Chapel at any point along life's journey. It exists, not as a particular circuit, but as a state outside of yourself—outside of space-time—that can happen at any time during your development. Many of the shocks that activate the transpersonal circuits can be exactly that—jarring to the nervous system and to the ego-self. These experiences can be very disorienting for some, propelling them into a chaotic, depersonalized state. Some may become trapped within it for years; others may enter and never come out the other side. Further, those who find the exit are not guaranteed progress or the experience of enlightenment. You may go in and out of the Chapel many times before being able to successfully progress in a collected or integrated manner.

Repressions Resurfacing

As consciousness broadens with increasing complexity, original repressions may come to conscious light, triggering ego collapse. When this occurs, there can be a regression and a return to primary processes of thought. From this can develop a lack of emotional flexibility and the possible emergence of "subselves" as coping mechanisms.

Disembodiment

Experiences of "leaving the body" can happen in this state. This may be for a number of reasons, including attempts at avoiding "karmic duty" or your "destiny"; over-thinking; or cognitive dissonance between individual spiritual experiences and religious indoctrination. Resistance, rigidity, or personal dissolution can result from hesitation to appropriately let go of the ego or surrender fully to incoming experiences.

SPIRITUAL EMERGENCIES

Dr. Stanislav Grof's work with psychedelics and the exploration of human consciousness notes ten key types of "spiritual emergencies" that may arise as you approach transpersonal realms:

- The shamanic crisis
- Episodes of unitive consciousness ("peak experiences")
- The awakening of kundalini
- Psychological renewal through return to center
- The crisis of psychic opening
- Past-life experiences
- Communications with spirit guides and "channeling"
- Near-death experiences
- Experiences of close encounters with UFOs
- Possession states

OBSESSIONS

Several "entrances" into this bardic in-between state have been proposed. As noted above, over-thinking can act as a catalyst for leaving your body. Obsessions can develop out of destabilizing shocks or traumatic events in an attempt to regain control over your life. While this may act as a temporary restorative action, it can also lead to "falling into the abyss." These obsessions can relate to many things—people, drugs, money, sex, ideas, religion, work, health, appearance, charitable causes, or social status or ego, to name just a few. People may become obsessed with the upper circuit shocks themselves, or with seeking out novel experiences or information—a sort of compulsive neophilia. This can escalate to such levels that you can spin into relatively short-lived sub-manic or manic episodes that end up consuming your resources. This results in a crash-and-burn scenario. At other times, an obsession can limit the scope of your experiences by accumulating so much force and inertia within your life that it stagnates decision-making. This can bring a deep immersion into maintaining day-to-day habits and routines.

Letting Go & Finding an Exit

Eventually the ego may realize it cannot win in the effort to maintain pre-egoic or dissolutioned states. It starts to divert its struggle against transcendent states toward its own resistances. As this happens, instincts are tamed and the ego "re-inhabits the body" to now deconstruct fears, defenses, repression, and aspects of the self-complex. Nisagadatta Maharaj says of this process that "the mind creates the abyss, the heart crosses it." Introspection and subsequent transference of findings to the conscious or subconscious can help to reestablish ground on which you can once again stand.

Reflections

How many of the above descriptions of spiritual emergency have you experienced firsthand?

Reflect on these spiritual emergencies and how they felt.

Reflect on a time(s) you have felt as if you have entered Chapel Perilous.

Try to identify people (real or fictional) who seem to be in or have gone through a Chapel Perilous experience/spiritual emergence/spiritual emergency. What did that look like and how did they get through it? How were they transformed, positively or negatively, from this experience?

Reflect on any tools, actions, steps, or thoughts that may have been helpful in re-establishing clarity and leaving Chapel Perilous.

Action Steps

Chapel Perilous can feel confusing and disorienting due to extraordinary experiences and/or overactive meaning-making faculties paired with insufficient ability to adequately question, integrate, and ground non-ordinary experiences and ideas.

Common signs may include: everything feels symbolic or "about you"; interpreting patterns or projecting meaning onto things with little-to-no corresponding basis in "reality"; interpretations of "reality" feel charged or threatening; feeling as though you're going crazy; certainty about non-veridical perceptions (these may oscillate); agency feels compromised (as though something external is controlling you); identity becomes fluid but unstable.

The exit at this point is not more insight and meaning-making, but re-anchoring the ego to consensus reality. Chapel Perilous ends when meaning-making becomes playful and curious again rather than scary, destabilizing, and damning. The exit is neither certainty nor disbelief, but sovereign authorship, embodiment, and choice. Here are Chapel Perilous exit exercises designed specifically for re-grounding, re-stabilizing meaning, and restoring agency after prolonged liminality, ontological shock, synchronicity overload, or identity destabilization.

Reduce Excessive Meaning-Making

If you are feeling overwhelmed by patterns and signs all around you, choose one object near you, describe it without metaphor (e.g., "This is a mug. It is ceramic. It holds liquid. It weighs about half a pound"). If symbolic thoughts arise, note them, but do not engage. Remind yourself, "Not everything is a message." Repeat this throughout the day when you find yourself feeling overwhelmed or confused by the "messages" you may be perceiving all around you. This gently disengages runaway Circuit 7 → Circuit 3 loops.

Lower Circuit Grounding

For a set period (24–72 hours minimum), reduce or pause divination, astrology, synchronicity tracking, symbolic interpretation, or other spiritually charged endeavors. Replace with neutral sensory input, routine tasks, grounding physical activities, predictable schedules, empirical thinking, and social support. Remind yourself: *"I am allowed to rest from meaning."* All circuits should work in balance and harmony. When there is destabilizing upper circuit imbalance, it can be helpful to counterbalance and ground into the lower circuits.

Containing Uncertainty

Instead of trying to resolve uncertainty, contain it. Consider, "There may be something I don't understand yet. I do not need to resolve it now. I can revisit it another time." Then just leave it with a mental bookmark you can return to. This prevents perseveration on something destabilizing, while remaining open to assimilating it in the future when you may be better able to metabolize it.

WHEN TO SEEK PROFESSIONAL SUPPORT

- Thoughts of wanting to harm yourself or others
- Increased paranoia
- Prolonged sleep disruption
- Excessive/disruptive feelings of fear about experiences rather than curiosity
- Reality testing weakens
- Meaning feels threatening or persecutory

It can be helpful to find a mental health professional with a transpersonal/psychospiritual background who may be better able to support individuals with unconventional worldviews.

CHAPTER 8

CIRCUIT 5: PLEASURE SEEKING, GETTING "HIGH," & ECO-CONSCIOUSNESS

CHAPTER SUMMARY

The fifth circuit marks a major transitional phase in psychospiritual perspective and development. Whereas most everyone in modern society imprints the first four circuits and develops them to some degree (barring significant trauma, inhibitory situations growing up, or cognitive impairment), this is not the case with the following four stages. The higher circuits can be thought of as explorations of transpersonal experiences. Each circuit entails greater and greater degrees of conscious control over previous imprints and aspects of Self.

CONSCIOUS SOMATIC EXPERIENCE

With fifth circuit activation, it becomes possible to develop a broader perspective of the world beyond the ego-self. With it you reach a level of intelligence and self-awareness that becomes more adept at conscious control and change of your body to best suit your needs or desires. For this reason, it has been called the "neurosomatic circuit." This is the unlocking of sensory and bodily consciousness. The first circuit relied on the body's experience focusing around survival, and the automatic functions of the body that maintain life. With C-5 activation, the emphasis again is placed on the body and the sensory experience, but now actively seeks and self-directs toward pleasurable endeavors for enjoyment rather than mere survival. It strives toward self-embellishment and ecstatic experiences that expand beyond the personal ego.

The body now becomes a vehicle of joy and rapturous experience—able to use the senses to explore the world for fun and pleasure. Pleasure can now act as its own reward.

In the Present Moment

Being present in the immediate moment is a major goal of meditative and mindfulness practices. With this comes the ability to let life happen around you and inside you without cultural value judgments—i.e., allowing yourself to be enveloped as part of an unfolding process. You begin to recognize the inherent flow of the universe, and that each entity exists within this flow. Neurosomatic consciousness has been described as "amotivational" with *"nothing to do, nothing worth doing...right where you are sitting now."* This circuit communicates outside of words; it is fully felt as an immersive sensory experience. Movements, gestures, dance, feelings, posture, and attitude are the primary means of communication.

Means of Sensory Intelligence

Sounds are one of the most direct ways of accessing sensory intelligence. For this reason, music can have a strong impact in a way that words cannot. It is felt rather than a drawn conclusion. The act of listening communicates directly to somatic intelligence, and the act of creating aural experiences can lead to altered or ecstatic states. This enhanced sensory sensuality can apply to the whole body with full neurosomatic activation.

Negative-To-Positive Sensitization

Many accounts by shamans, medicine men, or spiritual individuals who have activated the neurosomatic experience report first experiencing a negative-to-positive sensitization upon unfolding. Before reaching a stage of open receptivity to bliss states, you might first feel that you are losing hold of your sense of Self. This can be accompanied by the sense of terror of personal annihilation. There can be an abrupt fear as the Self that you have known all your life becomes deconstructed, or suddenly feels without any distinct significance. Not everyone goes through this process, however—some are lucky enough to bypass it and directly access neurosomatic pleasure. A positive neurosomatic imprint re-enforces the body as a source of pleasure and grace, to be in—and rejoice in—the present moment, and to become fully enraptured by it.

SENSUAL AVERSION

A negative neurosomatic imprint can, in the long term, result in experiencing the opposite of neurosomatic pleasure—sensory experiences are filtered through a reality tunnel that renders them unpleasant or even painful. Thus, sensory experiences may be avoided rather than sought out. The body may be rejected as a source of discomfort or pain. Sensuality may be seen as anxiety-producing and uncomfortable. Perceptions can distort into a nightmarish reality. Light can become particularly painful, overwhelming, and terrifying. In some negative imprints, unpleasant experiences may seem to be related to a sort of mind control—you do not perceive these negative experiences as originating from within, but as the workings of an external force.

SOCIETAL BACKLASH

A newfound sense of the body as a source of pleasure, joy, and fun can lead to troubles within the socio-political environment. Self-directed goals of personal gain or enjoyment may not fall within cultural expectations. As such, you may feel inclined to disregard, or work counter to, the social structure to focus on individual fulfillment. An example of this is the counterculture movement of the 1960s, where focus was put on breaking away from the culturally restrictive morals of the time for more worldly and hedonistic pursuits such as love, sex, altered states, spirituality, connecting with and protecting the environment, and larger scale group consciousness through communal gatherings, festivals, music, and art. It was an attempt at large-scale neurosomatic activation.

It is important to be aware that these approaches can be seen as a "social threat" as it challenges the established expectations of interpersonal morals and norms. This threatening nature remains whether the outcome and outlook are ultimately of benefit. The fear of change (neophobia)—or an unwelcome self-awareness—can cause a great deal of reactionary anxiety or anger in others. As such, the criticism can be quite harsh. You may be called "self-centered" or "selfish"; it can even elicit physical violence. It can, after all, be seen by others as a threat to the foundation of their own identity or belief structure(s).

"Getting High"

The neurosomatic circuit, by definition, includes the nervous system's ability to get "high" in many different ways, and to find methods to reach blissful states. These include meditation, yoga, breathwork, endorphins, etc. To form a strong neurosomatic circuit, you give yourself permission to fully indulge your inner desires and to know what those desires are—temporarily, at least.

This must be established to continue into further stages of complexity that become progressively more subjective and subtle. These demand a firm ability to look inward with integrity and assurance that your thoughts and feelings are trustworthy beacons of direction. Intuition becomes clearer the more you become receptive, aware, and attentive to it.

Too Much of a Good Thing

C-5 actions can be self-serving in the interest of growing self-awareness. This can become problematic, however, if it is so over-embellished that it becomes a hindrance to your life and progress—neurosomatic excess. It can become easy to get so caught up in (or even addicted to) states of rapturous bliss that it becomes the end goal instead of a means to an end—personal growth. When bliss itself becomes the goal in the long term, it may lead to laziness and personal disorganization, potentially leading to unhealthy psychological states. It becomes necessary to develop the ability to make your own value judgments and self-regulate your time in bliss to avoid excess/treadmilling. Such is the path of the Bodhisattva in Buddhism.

Some people go through a period in which they may become too "blissed out," too spacey, disoriented, or they don't feel "all together" as their self-dependence unfolds and personal ego softens. The increase in endorphins and reward neurotransmitters (like dopamine) during all of this feeling good can also feed into this sort of spaced out sensation. It is important not to get stuck in this stage. At some point, to interact within society, the sense of Self must be established again to come down from the cloud of euphoria you've been floating around on, but with the knowledge that you can readily return when appropriate.

Abstraction

Thinking can become more abstract with neurosomatic activation. Linear thought forms may give way to less linear or more holistic concepts.

Conscious Autonomic Control

Once hedonic states associated with this circuit have been integrated and self-awareness becomes more refined, you become capable of taking conscious control of and regulating autonomic functions and involuntary reflexes. Control of the breath is one of the easiest places to start this process. Consciously slowing down or deepening the breath, has a systemic effect on everything from blood perfusion, muscle restrictions, and anxious mental states. When you become anxious, the breath tends to become restricted into a feedback loop of what the brain interprets as mild strangulation. Willfully deepening the breath can break this pattern.

EXPANSION OF LOVE

Neurosomatic intelligence also brings about a broader sense of love that extends beyond the singular Self and is no longer limited to those with whom you have direct interactions. There develops an expansive, boundary-breaking love of those you may have never met—a sense of love for all people, and often, all things. Others are seen as an extension of yourself and the realization that we are all of one ilk, one family, one species, and one planet coexisting as a superorganism. This expansion of love, for both Self and others, strengthens the heart. Fear fades away with the development of self-reliance and the ability to stand up and embody who you really feel you are.

SEXUALITY AS A VEHICLE TO ALTERED STATES

Sexuality can play a significant role in neurosomatic activation and experiences. Through the active prolonging of the sexual experience without achieving orgasm, the senses become heightened, and ecstatic altered states of consciousness can be achieved. Such methods have a long history—Tantric and Daoist sexual practices promote prolonging orgasm or abstaining from orgasm altogether. Some practices promote the conservation of ejaculate by males whereby control of bodily sensations and functions achieve a body-wide orgasm or energetic release without ejaculation. By these means you can utilize the pleasure of sexual activity and orgasm to achieve higher spiritual states.

CHARISMA

Personal charisma can also be cultivated in this circuit. You may find the ability to act effortlessly, and give total, undivided attention to your unique nature. There develops an increased awareness of your influence on others, an appreciation of the relational dynamic, and a newfound role within the grand universal play in which we all find ourselves.

AESTHETIC DEVELOPMENT & AWE

Awe has been defined as consisting of (1) an appraisal of vastness and (2) a need to accommodate that perception of vastness into existing mental structures. Additionally, the experience of awe has been further broken down into the following five qualities:

- Threat
- Beauty
- Exceptional ability
- Virtue
- The supernatural

The most common triggers of awe are nature and art. A well-known awe-inducing experience is known as "the overview effect." This is the experience people report upon viewing Earth from orbit or outer space. In such states of awe, the two psychological traits of "openness to experience" and "absorption" are most associated with spiritual experience (absorption has been observed to be the most predictive). Absorption is defined as "an openness to inner experiences as well as the capacity to have your attention engaged to the point that everything fades away from your awareness."

FLOW STATES

Based on the work of Mihaly Csikszentmihalyi, Ph.D., "flow" has been said to have eight characteristics:

- Complete concentration on the task
- Clarity of goals and reward in mind with immediate feedback
- Transformation of time (speeding up/slowing down)
- The experience is intrinsically rewarding
- Effortlessness and ease
- A balance between challenge and skills
- Actions and awareness are merged, losing self-conscious rumination
- A feeling of control over the task

It may be characterized by the complete absorption in a task where action and consciousness seem to melt together. It becomes simultaneously demanding of high concentration while feeling effortless and immensely enjoyable. This can be considered a trait of C-5 consciousness.

NEUROBIOLOGY

Brain images of people during meditation have been compared to those without meditation experience. Findings tend to show that long-time meditators have thicker frontal lobes, that meditation practice produced functional and structural brain changes, particularly in areas involved in self-awareness and self-regulation. Meditation and yoga practices have also been associated with reduced amygdala volume. It has been noted that areas of the attentional network, such as the prefrontal cortex (PFC), are involved in attention-focused tasks that may elicit non-ordinary or ecstatic states of consciousness including prayer and ritual practices.

While these practices may demonstrate thicker neural connections, "transient hypofrontality theory" speaks of a temporary reduction in activity in the frontal regions of the brain. This may be found in experiences such as dreaming, endurance running, meditation, daydreaming, hypnosis, and various drug-induced states. This temporary downregulation may lead to experiences that feel overwhelming or out of your control as well as accounting for flow states.

It has been proposed that the dopaminergic system in the PFC relates to the personality trait of "openness/intellect," which reflects characteristics of cognitive exploration, including tendencies to be imaginative, curious, perceptive, artistic, and intellectual. This may be the neural correlate of neophilia—an inclination to seek out new experiences and information, with the dopaminergic reward system providing satisfaction or pleasure from these pursuits.

Relating to awe and absorption experiences, the medial orbitofrontal cortex (mOFC), which is known to be involved in the perception of rewarding stimuli, has been shown to become more activated when seeing or experiencing "beautiful" artwork (i.e., beautiful according to the observer's subjective taste). Experiences of awe have been correlated with reduced activation of the default mode network (DMN). Absorption experiences are correlated with increased activation in the following brain areas: superior frontal gyrus (SFG), the bilateral middle temporal gyri (MTG), posterior cingulate cortex (PCC), the lateral occipital cortex, and the temporal pole.

CHAPTER LESSONS

- Role of awe/flow
- Rapturous experiences
- Pleasure-seeking
- Hedonic engineering
- Endorphins and the endocannabinoid system
- Ego remaining intact, but "larger": ego expansion
- Conscious control of activation of sensory/body experiences
- Dopamine/reward centers

GOALS

- Consider/explore how the body's sensory system can be used as a tool for self-knowledge and growth
- Consider and recognize potential personal C-5 disharmonies and imbalances
- Explore multiple models that may describe aspects of C-5 intelligence (awe, flow, meditation, reward systems, tantra)
- Consider ways that may improve or maximize your C-5 intelligence

QUALITIES OF CIRCUIT 5 DYNAMICS

BALANCED CIRCUIT 5 ENERGY

- Ability to discriminate between truth and untruth
- Content, centered; enthusiasm for life

- Feeling of connection or love with humanity and nature
- Can live in the present, meditate, and experience divine energy
- Great sense of timing
- Musically or artistically inspired; may be overwhelmingly prolific
- Sexual: can manifest incredible sexual/sensual energy, or abstain without great effort
- May choose to redirect sexual energy into creative endeavors (e.g., music, art, etc.)

Excessive Circuit 5 Energy

- Arrogant, self-righteous, dogmatic
- Loquaciousness or silence used as a means of control/attention
- Spaced-out, ungrounded, selfish
- Inability to put great thoughts into action
- Addictive
- Lack of personal accountability
- Sexual: preoccupied, unconsciously "macho"; may prefer partners who can be dominated or manipulated

Deficient Circuit 5 Energy

- Timid, quiet, holds back, scared, confused
- Inconsistent, unreliable
- Lack of creativity
- Weak, unable to express thoughts
- Can be devious or manipulative
- Sexual: can't relax; conflict with religious/moral raising; afraid of sex

REFLECTIONS

Core theme: Pleasure for the sake of itself, playfulness, creativity, joy, ecstasy

Imprint age: Nonlinear

Mantras: *"Pleasure does not require permission." "Beauty is all around." "I'm allowed to feel joy." "Creativity flows through me."*

Reflect on a time you felt fully immersed in a moment/activity/flow.

Are there any particular activities that you have found that help you get into a "flow"?

Reflect on a time in your life you have experienced bliss or a "rapturous" experience.

What physical activity/sensory experiences are most pleasurable to you?

What, if any, experiences/activities have you had or used to get "high"? Did/do you enjoy it? Why? Be specific about how it made you feel.

How could you feel these flow/rapturous/pleasurable states more often?

Why do you think the hippie culture of the 1960s lost momentum?

Have you ever felt like you lost control over your body/sensations? Was there something that worked to regain control?

Describe what it feels like to be "high" or "euphoric."

Consider visual or auditory stimuli that make you happy. Do you have a song that makes you feel joyful when you hear it?

Do you have a favorite/happy food?

Try to identify people (real or fictional) who embody quintessential C-5 characteristics. What are their strengths and flaws?

____

____

____

____

____

____

What would the world look like if Circuit 5 was the primary circuit people operated from?

____

____

____

____

____

____

ACTION STEPS

Activities that allow you to feel and take conscious control of the body, or allow for states of awe or rapturous blissful states. Some examples may include:

- Ecstatic states
- Hatha Yoga, Zen meditation, Pranayama
- Tantra; prolonged sexual play without orgasm
- Endorphin-inducing physical exertion (e.g., runner's high)
- Floatation/isolation tanks
- Floating in a boat on a calm lake
- Pleasure-seeking activities
- Full body massage for pleasure alone
- Immersively listening to your favorite music with quality headphones
- Shared creation or playing of live music (e.g., ecstatic drumming)

- Virtual reality experiences that emulate psychedelic or overview effects
- Surround yourself with people who only make you feel good
- Awe-inspiring sights such as natural wonders
- Allow yourself to get lost in the moment/experience
- Wander aimlessly and/or allow yourself to lose track of time
- Try to remove "meaning" from life for a time—experience it as qualities and energies
- Cannabis, low dose psychedelic experiences
- Mantras, chanting, prayer, voicing, calling in joy

MICRO-PLEASURE SAFETY TRAINING

Circuit 5 often destabilizes because pleasure was once conditional, overwhelming, associated with escape, or followed by loss, shame, or withdrawal. This exercise teaches the body that small pleasures are safe.

Choose one subtle pleasant stimulus that is both enjoyable and grounding:

- The warmth of a mug
- The sound of rain or ambient music
- The texture of fabric
- A color in the room
- A gentle stretch

Stay with it for 10–20 seconds only. If escalation occurs, gently disengage. Say internally: *"I can experience pleasure and return."* Repeat 1–3 times.

This re-imprinting effect repairs Circuit 5/Circuit 1 coupling, prevents dissociation, craving, or intensity chasing, and builds trust in enjoyment as regulating, not destabilizing. As you become increasingly comfortable with micro-pleasures, give yourself permission to gradually indulge in more decadent pleasures.

AESTHETIC ATTUNEMENT

Many Circuit 5 injuries come from aesthetic or sensual suppression. Choose something you find beautiful (e.g., music, art, poetry, scent, dance). Before engaging, state inwardly, *"I do not need to justify enjoyment."* Let yourself enjoy it without analyzing why you like it, or trying to find a deeper meaning or purpose in the experience. If guilt, shame, or self-judgment arises, just notice it while still allowing your enjoyment to continue alongside it. Stay present in this experience for at least 1–2 minutes.

FLOW

Circuit 5 can become a dissociative refuge if not anchored. Engage in an activity that naturally invites flow: drawing, dance/slow movement, music, writing by hand (calligraphy, poetry, or other creative writing), rhythmic walking.

Set a timer before beginning so you can end deliberately rather than getting lost in this state as an escape. While in flow, occasionally notice and remind yourself, *"I am here now, and I will return."*

SENSORY RE-ASSOCIATION

This exercise can be helpful when pleasure feels unsafe or overwhelming. Choose a sense that feels least threatening (e.g., the smell of a calming essential oil), and pair it with grounding input: feet on the floor, hand on your chest, or deep breathing with long, slow exhales. Reinforce to yourself, *"This is enjoyable and safe."*

If activation increases, return your attention to your body immediately. You can try this exercise another time with a different sensory stimulus.

CIRCUIT 5 RE-IMPRINTING MEDITATION: SAFE PLEASURE

Dim the lights and choose a comfortable position, seated or lying down. This meditation is designed to re-train the nervous system to experience pleasure without compulsion, guilt, or being overwhelmed.

Begin by gently regulating your breath. Inhale naturally, and let the exhale be slightly longer than the inhale. Feel your body relax more deeply with each exhale.

Bring awareness to the simplest sensations: the weight of your body, the support beneath you, the temperature of the air, the steady rhythm of breath...

Now choose one experience of beauty that feels safe. Nothing intense, dramatic, or ecstatic, but something small. Your favorite color. A soothing song. A gentle scent. Warm water. A memory of warm sunlight on your skin. A soft texture. A quiet moment of comfort. A serene scene in nature, maybe by a waterfall, the ocean, somewhere peaceful and sacred...

Hold it lightly. As you do, notice what happens inside you. Do you soften? Do you tighten? Do you feel numb? Do you feel guilt? Do you want more? Whatever arises is welcome. You are just noticing...

Now allow yourself to receive the beauty of this experience for just a few seconds. Even just 10 seconds is enough.

Let it touch you...and then let it fade.

Notice: You are still here. Nothing has been demanded. Nothing has been lost.

Repeat this gently.

Invite the beauty back. Receive it for a few more seconds. And let it go.

As you do this, repeat inwardly:

> *"Pleasure can be gentle. I can feel joy safely. I do not need to justify enjoyment."*

If you notice an urge to intensify, bring yourself back to baseline. This is a safety practice.

Now find the smallest pleasant sensation available in the body: a warmth in the chest, a softening in the face, a slight ease in the belly, a release in the shoulders...

Let it be enough. Rest here for several breaths.

Before closing, let this land in your body: *Joy is welcome. Beauty is allowed. My body is an instrument of pleasure.*

Return awareness to the room. Feel the ground beneath you. Stay present in your body. Allow integration to continue quietly...

Circuit 5 Integration Questions
Weekly Reflection

- What did I learn about my pleasure, creativity, and sensuality this week?
- How has my relationship with enjoyment and desire shifted?
- What practices most supported my Circuit 5 activation?
- Where do I still numb myself, compulsively chase, or feel guilt around pleasure?
- What does my body need in order to experience pleasure as safe and nourishing?
- How is Circuit 5 health affecting my lower circuits?

Chapter 9

Circuit 6: Metaprogramming, Neuroplasticity, & Brain Change

Chapter Summary

Circuit 5 develops volitional control over body processes with the ability to be used to create aesthetically or sensorially pleasurable experiences. Similar change and control happen with Circuit 6 in the realm of mental processes, belief structures ("B.S."), and neural signaling.

"Metaprogramming" is a term derived from computer programming. Dr. Lilly used it in the realm of the psyche to describe when you become able to use "metacognition"—thinking about your thinking—to observe, reflect on, and modify conditioned mental and cultural "programs."

While it is possible to change opinions or behaviors without activating this circuit, the range of possibilities tends to remain limited to concepts based on Circuit 1–Circuit 4 dynamics and imprints. Culturally determined constraints on the range of thought patterns and consensus opinions still tend to heavily influence perception, scope of information, and subsequent reactions. People usually stay in line with instilled cultural biases until metaprogramming consciousness is accessed.

"In the province of the mind there are no limits."
—Dr. John C. Lilly

This sixth "metaprogramming" circuit is a pivotal point within the 8-circuit model. It potentially provides the means of personal psychospiritual development and healing, whether for yourself or in guiding others. Circuit 6 activation and function may also lie at the crux of many mystical, spiritual, and occult practices, as well as the exploration or spontaneous experience of many "non-ordinary states of consciousness" (NOSCs). The 8-circuit model offers a useful framework for these states, experiences, ideas, and related phenomena.

Neurorelativity

Circuit 6 awareness leads to a new perspective of others, with a deeper understanding of each having, perhaps similar, but completely separate viewpoints, thought patterns, and sets of experiences influencing how they see and operate within the world. While activation of this circuit does not inherently eliminate bias, it might allow for more relativistic viewpoints in which multiple thought patterns or models of reality can be simultaneously perceived, evaluated, and held. This can allow individual bias to become more conscious and softer. As such, this circuit is considered one of neurological relativism and of the multidimensional Self.

Internal Locus of Control & Self-Validation

In C-6 consciousness, thought patterns tend to become more problem-centered and detached rather than ego-centered. This comes with greater spontaneity, honesty, creativity, appreciation, and richness of emotion as self-expression seems to bloom. This may allow for heightened personal independence: i.e., you may no longer define yourself by a particular group dynamic or culture, but rather as a citizen of Earth. Fear and compulsiveness tend to decrease, and energies that were bound up in fear-based processes can be freed and put toward new processes of creativity and self-refinement. Validation becomes derived more internally and self-driven. You become better able to separate emotions from an event, and refrain from acting on them without repression: i.e., you become able to fully feel the response while stepping aside and not embodying or being consumed by the reaction.

REALITY TUNNELS & FILTERS

The human mind, through its early developments, constructs lenses of perception—"reality tunnels"—through which every experience is filtered to maintain an internal status quo—continually reaffirming constructed models of reality. Information not matching this model is generally ignored and remains unprocessed. Prior to activation of the sixth circuit, this filtering tends to be automatic and unconscious. With circuit six activation, the nervous system becomes aware of its active participation in this process.

RELATIONAL THINKING

Sixth circuit cognition emphasizes a more relational understanding, making connections between variables that are more interdependent and open. Relativism, change, and conflict become seen as a more accurate model of the world, so you may find yourself developing an increased tolerance—or even a preference—for ambiguity, uncertainty, paradox, and flux. Choices may be approached under the mindset of "whatever happens, happens" or "everything always works out, one way or another," trusting that the results will, ultimately, turn out fine.

EXPANDED OR EXTRA-SENSORY EXPERIENCES

As ego defenses loosen or dissolve, you may experience states of expanded perception. The refined sensitivity to internal and external processes via the nervous and sensory system begins to unfold. Given that a significant portion of brain activity is dedicated to constantly inhibiting activities, it would not be a huge leap to consider some of these "extra-sensory experiences" may be accessible at all times but our brains are continually filtering them out. Neuroimaging of NOSC and psychedelic states have demonstrated a temporary reduction of this inhibitory function. Children and animals are thought to possess these extrasensory abilities as they have little in the way of filters and blockages. However, they lack the ability to fully understand and use them to their full potential as a tool of self-development and conscious change. With Circuit 6 consciousness, you do.

DIFFERENTIATING PERCEPTION FROM PROJECTION

Differentiating genuine expanded perception from psychological projection may become a problem. As these can seem like subtle differences, it becomes important to take an honest introspective look at the experiences and how much of yourself is being put into them. Carrying too much emotional attachment can get in the way of genuine perception. You must learn to question and parse out what may be projection, while at the same time, grasping how all experience stems from the filter of your neurocircuitry. This is a thin line of differentiation.

COMFORT WITH CONTRADICTIONS

Contradictions and strange loops become more commonplace as your perspective broadens. As an awareness of internal contradictions within the psyche increases, you become increasingly able to discern and integrate these toward a more functional whole. Internal dichotomies may begin to break down—for instance, masculine and feminine parts of Self may become more accepted regardless of birth sex. What may have once been considered the more "unattractive" parts of Self may be met with greater acceptance, with an overall increase in self-esteem and decreased ego defenses. *"You can be anyone you want this time around."*

MISUNDERSTANDINGS & EPISTEMIC TRANSFORMATION

Attempts to convey these types of experiences can sound like irrational ramblings of nonsense to those who have never had multidimensional or "peak" experiences themselves. Personal transformation refers to experiences that change your preferences, perspectives, desires, or values. An "epistemic transformation" is defined as experiences that are impossible to imagine if you have not actually had such an experience. Activation of the metaprogramming circuit allows for such epistemic experiences.

RELATIONSHIP TO MYSTICAL, MAGICKAL, & OTHER SPIRITUAL PRACTICES

Throughout the millennia, many esoteric traditions have been used, devoted to the search for Self, spiritual development, and connection with and exploration of the deeper meanings of existence. These systems are designed to facilitate changes in the consciousness of their practitioners. Such changes can be easily and clearly explained within the framework of the 8-Circuit Model. These systems tend to be made up of more complex systems of self-exploration that may allow for de-programming and reimprinting (i.e., metaprogramming) that spans all circuits. Thus, the study and practice of ritual and magick may be used as a tool for the intentional rewiring of your nervous system. You can heal your past, transform your identity, and re-program potentially limiting or harmful belief systems; behavioral, emotional, and thought patterns; and responses at the core.

NEUROPLASTICITY

Neuroplasticity is the ability of the nervous system to change by reorganizing its structure, functions, or connections. It is the brain's ability to adapt. Neurotransmitters serotonin and oxytocin seem to be key factors in this process. Various activities can influence neuroplasticity. It can be increased by environmental enrichment, physical activity, hypoxia/ischemia, trauma, SSRIs, or serotinergic psychedelics. Neuroplasticity can be decreased by stress, corticosteroids, depression, aging, irradiation, alcohol, psychostimulants, and opiates.

NEUROBIOLOGY

Imaging of non-ordinary states of consciousness (NOSCs), and the field of study known as neurotheology have presented some evidence of what may be occurring in such states within the brain and nervous system. Belief in general—whether religious or nonreligious—has been associated with greater activation in an area of the front of the brain called the ventromedial prefrontal cortex (vmPFC), while the neural correlates of religious beliefs seem to involve brain areas relating to theory of mind, emotional regulation, abstract thought and processing, and imagery. Theory of mind relates to "the understanding that others have intentions, desires, beliefs, perceptions, and emotions different from your own, and that such intentions, desires, and so forth affect people's actions and behaviors."

Interestingly, "low levels of [dopamine], as found in Parkinson's disease, showed a tendency toward decreased religiosity. Additionally, activity in the nucleus accumbens, the primary brain region of dopamine release, was found to precede peak spiritual feelings." It has been argued that changes in the thalamus might be essential for changing a person's belief system and overall approach to life. There is some evidence that supports that altered thalamic function is associated with intense spiritual experiences. A combination of prefrontal and cerebellar functions helps in creating various probabilistic models of reality.

CHAPTER LESSONS

- Metaprogramming/metacognition
- Active, conscious brain change
- Neuroplasticity and brain network dynamics
- Ritual practices aimed at loosening/evaluating/changing belief systems

GOALS

- Consider/explore how belief structures and their rigidity may influence your view of and how you navigate reality in your daily life
- Consider any time you may have experienced an ontological shock that resulted in re-evaluation of previously held belief structures

- Consider/recognize any potential imbalances or disharmonies in your 6th circuit.
- Explore multiple facets and models of Circuit 6 intelligence
- Consider ways you may take to loosen or break out of rigid, prohibitive, or detrimental belief structures

QUALITIES OF CIRCUIT 6 DYNAMICS

BALANCED CIRCUIT 6 ENERGY

- Charismatic; master of yourself
- Access to the "source of all knowledge"
- Experiences "cosmic consciousness"
- Non-attachment to material things or the fear of death
- Sexual: may experience Self as androgynous, no longer needing another person as it "distracts one's inner bliss." Celibacy may be a natural but unnecessary choice

EXCESSIVE CIRCUIT 6 ENERGY

- Egomania, pride
- "Psychic arrogance"
- Over-intellectualization
- Authoritarian, manipulative
- Religiously dogmatic
- Static and inaccurate interpretations of events; personal fears
- Recurring nightmares and delusional fantasies

DEFICIENT CIRCUIT 6 ENERGY

- Non-assertive
- Undisciplined
- Oversensitive to the feelings of others
- Afraid of success
- Inability to distinguish ego from higher Self

REFLECTIONS

Core Theme: True Will/life's purpose, personal autonomy, free will

Imprint Age: Nonlinear

Mantra: *"I am whatever I believe myself to be." "I can change myself at will." "Validation comes from within."*

Reflect on a time you had to restructure your thinking after being presented with new information; or you discovered that a belief you held no longer served you.

Describe any thought patterns or beliefs you currently feel that may inhibit or prohibit you from more happiness.

Where did you come to believe these ideas?

Is there room to work on changing this belief and cultivating more happiness? List 2 or three steps you can take toward this.

Where did most of your current beliefs come from?

Try to identify people (real or fictional) who embody quintessential C-6 characteristics. What are their strengths and flaws?

What would the world look like if Circuit 6 was the primary circuit people operated from?

ACTION STEPS

Activities that allow yourself to become consciously aware of your internal processes, thoughts, and behavioral patterns, and actively manipulate or redefine these processes.

- Sensory deprivation
- Raja Yoga
- Self-hypnosis
- NLP
- Chanting or ecstatic dance/drumming
- Ritual/magickal practices; tantra or "sex magick"
- Neidan/Daoist internal alchemy practices
- Extra Sensory Perception (ESP)/psi practices
- Ajna visualizations

THE OBSERVER: SELF-AWARENESS EXERCISE

Sit quietly and notice: *I am aware of my experience.*
Now add one line: *"I am aware from inside the body."*

Bring attention to:

- the weight of your legs
- the temperature of your hands
- the pressure of your jaw or tongue

Continue observing thoughts, emotions, and sensations. Make it a habit to tune into your body throughout the day to increase self-awareness rather than operating on autopilot.

BELIEF DECONSTRUCTION

Write one core belief as a sentence, then answer the following questions (do this with as many core beliefs as you can identify):

- Where did I learn this?
- When is it useful?

- When does it fail?
- What belief could I try on experimentally instead?

RE-WRITING INTERNAL SCRIPTS

This exercise is to help you identify beliefs you didn't choose. Write ten statements you were trained to believe, explicitly or implicitly, about:

- Money
- Love
- Power
- Sex
- Success
- Spirituality
- Authority
- Emotions
- Your body
- What makes someone "good"

Examples:

- "Don't be too much."
- "Safety comes from pleasing."
- "Work is what makes you worthy."
- "If you relax, you'll lose everything."
- "Spirituality must look a certain way."

For each, answer:

- Who installed this? (family, school, religion, media, subculture)
- What did/does it protect?
- What did/does it cost?
- Does it still serve me and do I consent to running it now?

The re-imprinting theme here is, *"I can uninstall what I did not choose."*

YOUR FAMILY DOCTRINE

Answer the following questions to explore the "unspoken commandments" of your family system. Use this format:

- "In this family, you must ______."
- "In this family, you are punished for ______."
- "In this family, love is earned by ______."
- "In this family, people like us do not ______."
- "In this family, the worst thing you can be is ______."

Then consider:

- What did this doctrine produce in me?
- What part of me still obeys it?
- What would I believe if I had never learned this?

Now reflect that *"I can honor where I came from without remaining under its law"* and identify what you would like to discard or transform. How would these changes affect your life and sense of self?

MEDIA DEPROGRAMMING

Identify which desires are yours vs. implanted. List 5 things you have wanted intensely in life. For each, ask:

- Did I want this before I saw it modeled?
- Who benefits if I want this?
- What identity does it promise me?
- What fear/anxiety does it soothe?
- What would I want if no one could ever see it?

Now repeat to yourself, *"My desire is mine when it makes me feel more alive, not more approved by others."* Identify what else you might desire or how you might live differently if you were living only for you without the influence of others.

The re-imprinting theme here is, *"I reclaim my wants."*

THE SHAME MAP

To find the places your culture still lives inside you, make a list of the things you feel shame around, even if you "don't believe in shame." Then label each shame with its origin:

- Family shame
- Religious shame
- Gender-role shame
- Class shame
- Academic/status shame
- Sexual shame
- Spiritual shame
- Body shame

Then ask:

- Who taught me this?
- What was it designed to control?
- What would I do if this shame disappeared?

Re-imprinting reflection: *"Shame is not my truth. It's an external social construct I believed in and gave away my power to. It can no longer influence or control me. I take my power back without apology."*

THE AUTHORITY EXORCISM

This exercise is designed to remove internalized voices of authority. Identify the voices of at least three authority figures you carry. Examples:

- A parent
- A teacher
- A religion
- An ex
- A political ideology
- An institution
- A celebrity or other idol

For each, write:

- What it says
- What it rewards
- What it punishes
- What it fears

Then write your response as your adult self: *"Thank you. I no longer outsource my mind to you."*

The re-imprinting message here: *"I am the authority in my inner world."*

BELIEF DISSECTION

Break a core belief down to parts. Choose one belief that shapes your life (e.g., *"I'm hard to love"; "People can't be trusted"; "If I'm not exceptional, I'm nothing"; "I must be useful to be safe.")*

Now dissect it:

- The first time I remember believing this:
- Who benefited when I believed it?
- What did it help me to survive?
- What does it prevent me from receiving now?
- What belief would be truer and kinder today?

Re-imprinting reflection: *"A belief can be honored for its service and retired."*

REALITY TUNNEL SWAP

Think of this practice as an experiment. When you alter the lens through which you view the world, you can notice how that affects how you feel, what you think, how you act, and other outcomes.

Pick one situation (e.g., a conflict, a fear, a desire) and write three interpretations:

1. The inherited interpretation (family/culture default)
2. The trauma interpretation (protection strategy)

3. The liberated interpretation (chosen consciously)

Then ask:

- Which interpretation expands my agency?
- Which one shrinks it?

The re-imprinting mantra here is, *"I choose the reality tunnel that supports life."*

THE MYTH YOU ARE LIVING

Identify the story you're trapped inside. Write the myth of your life in five sentences, like a legend. Then name the role(s) you're stuck in (e.g., martyr, exile, chosen one, rescuer, cursed one, perpetual student, scapegoat, invisible one, orphan, black sheep, etc.)

Then rewrite the myth with a different role:

- The builder
- The witness
- The lover
- The sovereign
- The wanderer
- The healer
- The ordinary human

The re-imprinting message here is, *"I can re-imagine and re-write my own story."*

MAP VS. TERRITORY CHECK

The objective of this exercise is to prevent overidentification with any particular framework (including this one!). Choose a favorite model, system, or belief structure you use and ask:

- Where does this map fail?
- Who does it not work for?
- What does it oversimplify?

- What lived experience contradicts it?

Maps are most useful when lightly held. Robert Anton Wilson's idea of "model agnosticism" treats every worldview (e.g., scientific, spiritual, political, or conspiratorial) as a useful *lens* rather than final truth. It encourages you to stay flexible: trying on models, testing what they do to your perception, and letting them go when they become rigid or dogmatic.

Circuit 6 Re-Imprinting Meditation: The Inner Architect

Dim the lights and get comfortable, seated or lying down. You may wish to record this meditation with a soft, steady voice and quiet ambient music. Begin by regulating your breath: inhale gently, exhale slightly longer. Let the body soften. Feel the support beneath you. Feel gravity holding you. You are *here*.

Now notice: thoughts appear, sensations shift, emotions rise and fall...and you are aware of all of it. Something within you watches with presence. Rest there for a few breaths, just observing...

Now gently recognize that much of what you call "me" is not your actual essence, but conditioning, training, and adaptation... A nervous system that learned rules about what is safe, what is dangerous, what is allowed, what is punished, what must be hidden, what you must believe, and how you must behave. Without naming any specific story, let yourself feel the weight of those invisible rules. Repeat inwardly: *"I was trained and I can be retrained."*

Now bring attention to the felt sense of limitation. Not a specific fear, just the subtle tightness of identity. The invisible walls around what you think you can be. The automatic bracing... The reflexive shrinking... Just notice it without fighting.

Take a slow breath in. On the exhale, loosen one small degree. Not breaking. Not forcing. Just loosening. Again: inhale... exhale... loosen...

Now let awareness widen. Feel the space around your body. The room. The air. Sense that your nervous system can expand and contract, and you can influence that. Repeat:

"I can expand safely."
"I can contract safely."
"I can choose."

Now remember: you have changed before. Even slightly. You outgrew something. You healed something. You became braver. You stopped believing something. Let that be proof that you are not fixed.

Now feel this shift:

You do not have to believe everything you think.
You do not have to obey everything you feel.
You do not have to become the first story that appears.
You can keep experimenting with and changing your identity at will.
You have authorship.

Repeat slowly:

"I am not my conditioning."
"I am not my fear."
"I am not my role."
"I am awareness learning itself."

Now open upward, gently. Let identity soften at the edges. Let your name, your history, your personality become lighter for a moment. Notice what remains... Maybe quiet presence... Clear awareness. A stillness beneath thought. Rest there. No conclusions. No explanations. Just leaning into that quiet presence of Self.

Maybe you sense something larger than your personal story. A connection with ancestors... Your divine purpose... A subtle whisper from the spirit world... A numinous glimpse into another dimension of reality... Depending on your previous conditioning and belief system, this might feel entirely natural and normal, it may feel jarring and impossible, or it may feel somewhere in-between. Just notice without judgment how you respond to this experience.

Now return to the body. Place a hand on the chest or belly to ground yourself. Reflect on your experience and how you've returned with more freedom. Repeat:

> *"I can change."*
> *"I can reorganize."*
> *"I can evolve without force."*
> *"I return with expanded choice."*

Take your time. Feel the ground. Feel the room. Open your eyes slowly. Do not interpret yet. Let the nervous system absorb this quietly.

When you are ready to deepen into the meaning of your experience, reflect on what opened up, and/or what you felt resistance to. The key here is exploring your experience with curiosity, flexibility, and non-judgment.

Circuit 6 Integration Questions
Weekly Reflection

- What did I learn about my beliefs, mental models, and conditioning this week?
- How has my flexibility of perspective and self-authorship shifted?
- What practices most supported my Circuit 6 activation?
- Where do I still feel trapped in inherited stories or automatic thinking?
- What does my nervous system need to feel free, open, and capable of change?
- How is Circuit 6 health affecting my lower circuits?

CHAPTER 10

CIRCUIT 7: GENETICS, GLOBAL CONNECTION, & SYNCHRONICITIES

CHAPTER SUMMARY

Seventh circuit consciousness transcends the extent to which the ego is capable of influencing and shaping reality through personal efforts alone. As you shift from self-generated codes and symbols to a source that lies outside your individual nervous system, you enter the realm of synchronicities, numinous experiences, trans-conscious knowledge, and manipulation of your own genetic code.

This circuit acts as a broader recapitulation of the third circuit that emphasized logic, rationality, and deductive reasoning to build symbols and models of the world. For the seventh circuit, the symbols transcend time and culture. They play a role in making up much more than just the individual, but rather that of the entire species.

EPIGENETICS

The ability for the expression of specific genes to be altered or turned on and off is the realm of "epigenetics." It has been demonstrated that a number of factors can alter genetic expression including medications, foods, emotional trauma, environmental toxins, and generational trauma. If a person's great grandfather experienced a very traumatic event (e.g., war, genocide, or severe food scarcity), this has been shown to activate or deactivate certain genetic expressions that may be passed down through the genetic line. Tapping into this aspect of Self may open the possibility to make positive change and directly work with and through some of these deep generational traumas. Within Circuit 7 states, it is possible to become conscious of the role of the genetic makeup and common lineage of these experiences permeating through the species.

Neurogenetic Intelligence

The gene pool now becomes seen as a network connecting all humans at a cellular level—a common factor through which all can relate. From this forms the perspective of Self as a transitory node within the larger existence of the species. Awareness broadens with recognition of an even more intelligent entity beyond Self: Gaia, the concept of the planetary ecosystem acting as one interconnected living organism. Ideas such as the Eastern concept of "reincarnation" and "transmigration," or tales of self-refinement into a spiritual "immortal" also come into consideration here. Once you become awakened to an awareness of neurogenetic intelligence, it becomes apparent that the broader definition of Self or collective DNA/RNA intelligence will continue to carry on forever. For similar reasons, those tapping into neurogenetic intelligence may report experiencing a "past life" or "past lives."

Psychologically, this stage of development makes accessible the common elements shared amongst humanity across time and space. This can be called the collective unconscious of Jungian psychologists, the Akashic records of theosophists, or what Stanislav Grof refers to as "phylogenetic consciousness."

Transcendence of the Mundane

Personal development tends to shift from focusing on transcendence of mundane aspects of existence to more "spiritual" concerns. With this, the mental ego will often desperately try to avoid the concept of impending non-existence by creating new challenges in attempts to avoid facing the inevitable. The ego eventually succumbs, accepting the "nothingness." This causes a radical shift in directed energies now reaching outward for guidance and support from the external universal processes that envelops it. This shift can be reached by either the path of joy or the path of suffering as laid out in numerous esoteric traditions. Whether the initial motivation stems from ecstasy or despair does not make a difference in the end—both lead to transcendence of ego to grasp the underlying "Absolute Reality."

ALTERED STATES

As circuit 7 intelligence increases, ordinary awareness becomes destabilized, and non-ordinary states of consciousness (NOSCs) are cultivated in greater and greater frequency. These states and experiences are characterized by feelings of ecstatic unity, the transcendence of time and space, a sense of internal authority, paradoxicality, and indescribability. Perceptions of time can become plastic, seeming to slow down, speed up, stretch out, or not exist at all. Sensory perceptions and the sense of body fade away as consciousness becomes enraptured in bliss and single-pointedness. Over time, sensations, feelings, the sense of Self, and space-time become abandoned. No longer identifying as an independent observer, you become an active participant of this process. All objects become seen as no longer constant—the only object of awareness that becomes recognized is that no true individual observer exists—only processes and representation.

ARCHETYPES

Circuit 7 is the realm of dream imagery and archetypal figures that are genetically present within the psyche of all of humanity. Archetypes are vague, underlying forms of archaic patterns embedded deep within species consciousness that universally permeate human existence regardless of culture, place, or time. These themes vary in their specific manifestations as each depiction is first filtered through the interpretations of the individual nervous system as well as through culturally ingrained notions of the nature of reality. Here dwell the archetypes of Jung's collective unconscious: gods, goddesses, angels, demons, the fae, elves, dwarfs, and other elementals or personifications of the DNA programs (instincts) that govern us and/or embody the forces of nature within and around us. We become able to visit the domain of mythological realities, fantastic landscapes, and abodes of the Beyond. Deep personal experiences of this realm may bring about the revelation that the images of the cosmos found in pre-industrial societies may not be based on superstition or primitive "magical thinking," but on direct experiences of alternate realities.

SYNCHRONICITY

As C-7 awareness arises, you may become more aware of increasing synchronicities within your life. The concept of synchronicity was coined by Carl Jung; he defined it as the co-occurrence of two or more meaningful events that are not causally connected, and which are not likely to occur by chance—an "acausal connecting principle." It can also describe a current psychic state that corresponds with an event that has not yet happened, but which can later be confirmed. They are considered convergences of seemingly unrelated coordinate points serving to develop depth and psychological significance.

NUMINOUS EXPERIENCES

Jung defined a "numinous experience" as a unique experience that is "inexpressible, mysterious, terrifying, directly experienced, and pertaining only to the divinity." It may be experienced as "the feeling of being in touch with divinity or God," or a "revelatory experience" entailing voices, visions, or epiphanies that seem to come from beyond yourself.

MYSTICAL EXPERIENCES

William James proposed four criteria to qualify as a "mystical experience":

- Ineffability: beyond your capacity to readily express it in language
- Noetic quality: insight that remains inarticulate
- Transiency: The experience tends to be brief and passing
- Passivity: The experience seems to happen to the experiencer who surrenders

The language of the mystics seems to fall into two categories:

- Statements of the logically impossible—the non-dualistic functioning of the transpersonal circuits *("Mysticism is neurogenetics expressed in pre-scientific symbols")*
- Statements of the "palpably untrue"—false mystics, cult leaders, and spiritual manipulators/exploiters

These states, and transitions toward self-transcendence, are said to not be attainable by desire or serious study alone. Although these factors must be in place to do so, it is said to be born through an "arduous psychological and spiritual process, and the liberation of a latent stage of consciousness." Experiential metaphors and imagery both hide and reveal The Ultimate. These mystical experiences, like the archetypal images, vary in accordance with cultural or subjective filtering or distortions.

AN ACTIVE PARTICIPANT IN THE PROCESS

With work and Circuit 7 consciousness, you may gradually come to recognize this subjective influence, and open up to your particular role in the makeup of reality. The world becomes understood according to non-Newtonian structuring that seems acausal, relativistic, holonomic, and interconnected throughout. As this happens more consistently, you may experience your relationship with reality as participatory, wherein your attention begins to have an effect on your environment. Meaning that has been placed on particular objects and concepts, become recognized as artificially created and only as meaningful as you make them. Improved access to memories, creativity, unhabituated attention, and enhanced sensory acuity may also become accessible.

SHIFT TO SELF-GUIDED DIRECTIVES

In the previous circuits, people may tend toward benevolent acts under the guise of altruism with underlying self-interest. Activation of the neurogenetic circuit, however, allows you to be enveloped by feelings of gratitude, loving kindness, generosity, and an effortless compassion for the humanity in all others. They are now experienced as inseparable from Self. Because of this, you may now truly accept others exactly as they are in every moment, as well as yourself and life in general, without a desire to exert control over any of it. This may be perceived by others as ambivalence or a lack of emotion, but the opposite may actually be the case as it results from an increased, widely-broadened emotional engagement with the world.

ISOLATION & SENSORY DEPRIVATION / IMMERSION

Non-ordinary states of consciousness become increasingly common with either decreased sensory input, or its opposite, sensory overload. In cases of sensory deprivation, the brain is left with only its own internal processes and neural landscapes to encapsulate awareness; it begins to generate its own hallucinations. This is the basis behind long-duration sensory deprivation tanks or dark room retreats where visual input is eliminated.

PRE/TRANS FALLACY

Conventional psychology equates mystical experiences with a form of regression into pre-egoic states. Integral philosophy refers to as this as "the pre/trans fallacy" in which trans-rational mystical experiences become erroneously equated with pre-rational or pre-symbolic states. Unfolding states may, however, involve a component of regression in the service of transcendence in which lower states become accessible to address negative imprints or imbalances. This clears the field, allowing for optimal ego transcendence. To the experiencer, however, distinguishing these points becomes moot as it is experienced as an acausal, interwoven process.

NEUROBIOLOGY

There has been some research—and speculation—on the neurobiology of synchronicities. Increased levels of dopaminergic activity seem to motivate a search for, and observation of more patterns. Dopamine has shown linkages to extraversion, positive affect, openness to experience, broad thinking, and mental flexibility. And disruptions in areas of the brain that are responsible for language and abstract thought may make frames-of-reference more malleable to change. Thirdly, there seem to be changes in activity in the limbic system, in particular, the amygdala.

While numinous experiences become difficult to pin down neurobiologically, there exist some findings into neural correlates. To the brain, experiencing the presence of a higher being or entity may not be that different from experiencing the presence of another person. Brain regions typically implicated in social interaction, and activated during numinous experiences include the medial frontal and inferior parietal areas. Some evidence points to increased activity in the prefrontal cortex associated with the increased focus of attention; however, one of the common findings in brain scans is a decrease in frontal lobe function.

The noetic quality of a mystical experience has been proposed to have an association with both limbic system areas (such as the hippocampus, which is involved in memory) and the thalamus, which acts as a hub for the higher order processing of more general cognitive data among multiple cortical regions. Recent psychedelic research has begun looking at the claustrum region of the brain for contributing a possible "switchboard" role between brain networks that support perception, memory, and attention.

CHAPTER LESSONS

- Synchronicity
- Archetypes/transcultural symbolism
- Global consciousness
- Transcendence of language/gestalts
- Generational and cultural trauma; global suffering
- Epigenetics
- Collective unconscious; Akashic records
- Déjà vu
- Lucid dreaming/astral projection with the individual sense of Self intact
- Oracles and divination

GOALS

- Consider/explore how global and genetic/transgenerational information can be accessed and used as a means of self-knowledge or growth
- Consider/recognize any potential imbalances or disharmonies in your seventh circuit
- Explore multiple schools of thought /lenses that may describe Circuit 7 intelligence (Jungian psychology, oracle/tarot decks, esoteric/mystery schools)
- Consider ways that may improve or maximize your Circuit 7 intelligence
- Consider ways to hack your epigenetic expression

QUALITIES OF CIRCUIT 7 DYNAMICS

BALANCED CIRCUIT 7 ENERGY

- Receptive to synchronicities, patterns, and mystical states
- Feelings of spiritual sanctuary, faith, and inner peace
- Ability to work on and heal generational trauma patterns
- Ability to transcend the laws of nature; "miracle worker"
- Access to the unconscious and subconscious
- Ability to leave and return to the body at will in full consciousness

EXCESSIVE CIRCUIT 7 ENERGY

- Constant sense of frustration, hypersensitivity
- Anxiety, confusion, feeling out of control, destructiveness
- Lost in imagination, spaced out, desire to escape reality
- Unrealized power-status
- Mental-emotional imbalances: psychosis, depression, bipolar
- Frequent migraine headaches
- Sexual: sometime passionate, sometimes distant

DEFICIENT CIRCUIT 7 ENERGY

- No spark of joy; lack of spiritual connection
- Lack of "vision"
- Feeling of uselessness, no meaningful direction in life
- Confusion, apathy, unable to make decisions
- Alienation, isolation, boredom, depression
- Close-mindedness, negative self-image, introversion
- Catatonic

Reflections

Core Themes: Ancestral memory, synchronicity, extrasensory/exceptional abilities, astral projection, entity encounters

Imprint Age: Nonlinear

Mantra: *"Something ancient lives through me." "I trust meaningful coincidence." "My perception is wider than I was taught." "My awareness can move beyond my body and return safely."*

List any C-7 methods have you tried/experienced?

____

____

____

____

____

____

Have you ever had a lucid dream or experienced astral projection? Describe this experience.

____

____

____

____

____

____

Have you ever had an experience of feeling generational/racial/cultural trauma? If so, describe this experience.

____

____

____

____

What has your experience been with the use of oracle/divinatory tools/systems?

Have you ever experienced déjà vu? Describe this experience as a materialistic artifact of brain-wave misfiring. Then describe this experience as a form of clairsentience.

Describe one or more times you've experienced synchronicity (meaningful coincidences).

Compare any similarities among any of the above experiences and how they differ.

____

____

____

____

____

____

In light of epigenetics, how might you change your life choices to create a better future for you, your kin, the future of human civilization, and planet Earth as a whole?

____

____

____

____

____

____

Describe aspects/characteristics you share with every other human on Earth—make the longest list you can.

____

____

____

____

____

____

Language—write a poem describing the difference between how you want to see the world and how things currently are.

____

____

____

Describe any experience you may have had of a "higher voice." Consider this experience as if it were a hyper-dimensional entity; or your ancestors; or gods/goddesses or God; or your Self.

Try to identify people (real or fictional) who embody quintessential C-7 characteristics. What are their strengths and flaws?

What would the world look like if Circuit 7 was the primary circuit people operated from?

ACTION STEPS

Activities that open your nervous system to a broader spectrum of sensory perception and experience include:

- Holotropic Breathwork
- Kundalini yoga; crown chakra meditations
- Meditation
- Hemisync and other binaural/brain hemisphere balancing technologies (e.g., Hemi-sync)
- Deep brain stimulation
- "The God Machine" (i.e., temporal lobe magnetic stimulation)
- Attentiveness to synchronicities
- Attempt to eliminate sense of Self by covering all mirrors for a week
- Vow of silence—communicating by other means: writing, gestures, eyes
- Oracle/divinatory practices: tarot, yijing *(I Ching),* runes, etc.
- Create a family/lineage tree
- Bonus: expand this lineage tree tracing back to pre-hominid ancestors— primates, mammals, fish, fungi, bacteria, etc.
- Create your own language/alphabet/symbol system

ANCESTRAL THREAD RECALL

Write 3 traits you recognize in your family line that feel older than you (e.g., a gift, a wound, a repeating theme). For each, answer:

- Where do I feel this in my body?
- How does it show up in my relationships?
- If this pattern could speak, what would it say it needs?

The message here: *"I honor my lineage by healing its wounds and honoring its gifts."*

ANCESTRAL REPAIR LETTER

Write a letter from your future self to your lineage. It should include:

- What you understand now
- What you refuse to carry forward
- What you're choosing instead
- What you're grateful for
- What ends with you

Close with *"I keep the wisdom. I release the wound."*

SYNCHRONICITY: PATTERN TRACKING WITHOUT OBSESSION

The goal here is train signal detection + discernment. For 7 days, record synchronicities in a simple log:

- What happened?
- What did it feel like?
- What was I thinking about right before it occurred?
- What choice did it invite?
- Did acting on it improve my life?

Reflect on if/how this makes you more awake, more kind, more honest, more aware, and more aligned. Remember, *"A sign is useful when it helps me live a more meaningful life and make better choices."* If noticing patterns and coincidences in your life becomes overwhelming or disruptive, engage in C-3 or other lower circuit activities to ground yourself and reality test your experiences.

INTUITION DEVELOPMENT

Pick one domain you already sense strongly:

- People's emotions
- Energetic "vibes"
- Precognition

- Subtle body sensations
- Sudden knowing
- Feeling watched/presence detection

For one week, do this daily:

- Write what you sense (one sentence):
- Write how confident you are (0–10):
- Write what you actually know vs what you're interpreting:
- Later, record what turned out to be true:

Entity Encounters

If you've had entity contact (dream, psychedelic, astral, meditation, spontaneous), write:

- What happened (facts only)
- What I felt in my body
- What the presence seemed to want
- What happened afterward (energy, mood, life impact)

Now answer:

- Did this increase my clarity or confusion?
- Did this increase my agency or reduce it?
- Did this encourage dependency or empowerment?
- Did it respect my boundaries?

If you are attracting negative entities, that may be a sign of trauma (personal or ancestral) or imbalance in other circuits. Assess where there may be wounding, weakness, or imbalance before pursuing further C-7 work (unless you are working with healing C-7 imbalances).

Circuit 7 Re-Imprinting Meditation: The Thin Veil

Dim the lights and get comfortable, seated or lying down. You may wish to record this meditation in a soft, steady voice with quiet ambient music.

Begin by regulating your breath: inhale gently, the exhale slightly longer... Let the body soften. Feel the support beneath you as you deepen into relaxation.

Now notice your awareness as thoughts move... sensations shift... emotions rise and fall... and something in you observes it all...

Now let yourself remember something simple: human beings have *always* had non-ordinary experiences—dreams, visitations, synchronicities, precognition/sudden knowing, deep ancestral emotion, encounters with symbols or otherworldly entities that feel alive. This is not new. This is part of the human nervous system.

Repeat inwardly:

"I am not alone. This is part of the human experience."

Now bring your attention to the deeper layers of You—the older layers. Not just your personal memories, but the inherited patterns that live in your DNA: instincts, reflexes, fears, longings, intuitions. You do not need to understand or explain them. You only need to feel that you are more than one lifetime of information.

Refocus on the breath. Let the body listen...

Now imagine your awareness like a lantern. You can aim it. You can widen it. You can dim it. You can bring it home. You are not helpless in the face of the unseen. You have choice.

Repeat inwardly:

"I can open safely."
"I can close safely."
"I can return fully."

Now let your awareness widen, just slightly, as if you are sensing the space around you, not only the body. Feel the air. The room. The quiet field of perception. Notice if you sense anything subtle: a presence, a mood, a pattern, any types of signal. You do not need to interpret your experience or force anything to happen. Just notice...

Now invite the Circuit 7 layer of mind—the layer that speaks in symbols, dreams, archetypes, and synchronicity. The layer that knows through feeling, image, and pattern.

Say inwardly:

> *"I am open and receptive to new experiences, yet I am willing to stay discerning."*

If a symbol arises, let it arise. If a memory surfaces, let it surface. If nothing happens, that is also okay. This is an opening, an initiation.

Now, gently, set a boundary and repeat inwardly:

> *"Only what supports my well-being is welcome. Anything else can pass by. My body is my home base to which I will return safely."*

Feel that boundary as the calm protector of the nervous system.

Now allow the possibility that your life contains meaningful patterns. Not because you are special (we all are in our own way), but because you are alive. Let yourself feel the intelligence of timing, the strange poetry of coincidence, the way the psyche and the world dance, intersect, and ripple forth.

Repeat:

> *"Life speaks in patterns."*
> *"I notice what repeats."*
> *"I take what helps, and I release the rest."*

Now rest for several breaths in quiet openness as you allow the channel to open and exist.

If you feel emotion (awe, grief, tenderness, fear), let it gently move through you. If you feel nothing, let that be okay, too.

Now begin to return. Feel the weight of your body. Feel the ground. Feel your breath. Bring one hand to the chest or belly.

Before closing, repeat slowly:

> *"My perception is wider than I was taught. I trust my discernment. I explore safely and return fully."*

Take your time as your awareness returns to your physical space. Open your eyes slowly. Silently sit with your experience and allow the insights and integration to happen quietly.

CIRCUIT 7 INTEGRATION QUESTIONS WEEKLY REFLECTION

- What did I learn about my ancestral patterns and deeper intuition this week?
- How has my relationship to synchronicity, archetypes, or expanded perception shifted?
- What practices most supported my Circuit 7 activation?
- Where do I still doubt, fear, or distort my deeper knowing?
- What does my nervous system need to explore the unknown with trust and discernment?
- How is Circuit 7 health affecting my lower circuits?

CHAPTER 11

CIRCUIT 8: NON-DUAL CONSCIOUSNESS, EGO DISSOLUTION, & THE DEATH EXPERIENCE

CHAPTER SUMMARY

The most expansive and complex circuit of consciousness may unfold with continued self-work or with some of the most intense shocks to your nervous system, including those tied to death and self-dissolution. With this, the universe itself may seem to come apart at the seams. As this is happening, you may feel a sense of eschatothesia—the feeling of the end of the world itself. Universe breaks wide open and becomes fully accessible as the individual Self seems to cease to exist as an isolated entity from everything else around them. A sense of henosis—a feeling of "oneness" with everything—emerges. The world is no longer seen as innumerable separate objects; these become recognized as constructs of your nervous system, and at their root, existing as a continuous ebbing and flowing of interconnection and interaction.

This description seems markedly similar to the concept of Indra's net as found in the *Avatamsaka Sutra;* Nirvana in Buddhism; Samadhi in yoga; the Satori of Zen; and the kingdom of heaven in Christianity. (Chinese descriptions tend to use terminology of negative structuring: "no-mind," "not-doing," and "not-existence.")

ONENESS WITH EVERYTHING

The sense of Self deteriorates to where no separation remains. To influence any part of it is to simultaneously influence the entire system. It is important to note that in some indigenous knowledge systems, the idea of self-loss loses any significance because the "Self" is seen as inherently connected to all things at all times, thus leaving nothing to lose.

THE DEATH OF DEATH

Concepts of death may be seen as irrelevant as you experience firsthand a grasping of the law of conservation of energy in which nothing ("no-thing") ever gets destroyed or created, only converted from one form to another. The perception becomes that we, at our essence, are already immortal, and physical death—as we tend to think of it—marks nothing more than a transition from one energetic form to another. No differentiation remains between living and dying as a localized consciousness, with death acting as a liberation from the confines of the nervous system and the constructs of space and time. With this, fear or anxiety surrounding the concept of death may be shed.

NON-ATTACHMENT

Desires and attachments similarly may dissolve as these things no longer seem to hold any significance beyond the temporary. As the ego becomes completely transcended, so too does self-driven interest and motives of further becoming; there may seem nowhere to go and there never was. All existed prior to awareness of it, and has been present and available the entire time. The universe is not empty; rather, it seems a boundless sea of potential that is waiting to be interpreted by tools—which, in the case of what we have discussed throughout this book, is the human nervous system.

INFINITE CO-INTELLIGENCE

Consciousness and information become perceived as a coherent co-intelligence that expands outward in all directions into infinity. The Self lies beyond the boundaries of space and time. The act of perceiving and interacting entails, and indeed demands, a duality—because the act of perception itself creates boundaries between the perceiver and the perceived. When consciousness reaches a certain level of expansiveness, however, any sense of Self ceases to exist. The perceiver, perceived, and the act of perception itself all cease to exist, leaving no dichotomous subjective/objective universe remaining.

CLEARING OF REPRESSION

Psychological coping mechanisms or restorative actions become cleared away as repression is no longer necessary. Feeling and perception are immediate and non-conflictive as a total psychic integration exists. That is, experience becomes immediately processed and integrated.

QUANTUM PHYSICS & QUANTUM CONSCIOUSNESS

Many attributes of these principles were once simply an intuitive "knowing" by the self-aware individual. They can now be found in descriptions in the field of quantum physics, its implications to our understanding of Universe, and its portrayal of the nature of "reality."

BELL'S THEOREM

No isolated systems, objects, or particles seem to exist throughout the universe. Any time a particle interacts with any other particle, the two create a bond through a process known as "quantum entanglement." This bond will never be broken, remaining from that point on, regardless of space or time between them. As these particles continue to interact with even more particles, a complex network of communication and interaction becomes created. This communication seems to occur instantaneously, or "non-locally," no matter how distant the particles may be in physical or temporal space.

WAVE/PARTICLE DUAL NATURE

The nature of reality depends on the method by which it is measured or perceived. By the same token, your sensory organs act as the instruments through which the world is experienced, and how they are used can influence your perception of reality. Every particle throughout the universe, under certain conditions, using certain instruments, can be measured as a solid object inhabiting a particular place in space with quantifiable dimensions. Under other conditions, using other instruments, this same "particle" does not act as a particle at all, but as a wave or vibratory function (a "process" rather than "thing"), lacking physical form. Reality and its underlying qualities, including the materiality of physical objects, become the responsibility and creation of the individual interacting with and interpreting it.

HEISENBERG UNCERTAINTY PRINCIPLE

Extending from the wave/particle dualistic nature, the observer acts as an active participant in the process of determining its attributes. As such, no firm boundary can be placed between them—they seem mutually dependent on each other, and inseparable. To this psychologically, the "Self" or the ego remains inseparable, and merely an extension of the world around them. Concepts of a separate Self become recognized as an illusion of our own making through the mechanisms of perception.

THE IMPLICATE ORDER

It's been theorized that Universe contains multiple layers of reality with varying degrees of complexity and organization (or lack thereof). The familiar material world contains physical objects that seem to adhere to standard Newtonian physics. This is referred to as the "explicate order." Behind all of this material "stuff" is what has been called the "implicate order" of "deep reality." It is made up of a yet to be observed undifferentiated ocean of energy, potential, or probability waveforms that transcends space, time, and causality. This implicate order permeates all space, yet cannot be directly perceived. Out of the implicate order, physical properties and events are said to "unfold" to make up the explicate order, to then enfold back into the implicate order of probability. From this, Universe becomes understood as a vast expanse full of information and potential.

The Holomovement

The holomovement is described as an infinite spectrum of implicate orders—an unbroken and undivided totality. It does not move from place to place (because location exists only relative to observation), but acts as a movement in terms of being a continually enfolding and unfolding process. Characteristics of the holomovement are:

- The universe of matter floats in a vast ocean of energy known as the implicate order
- This implicate order in some sense seems to be conscious or alive. As a result, all matter may also be considered alive/conscious
- The holomovement is a continuum of consciousness with matter composing the densest rung

Paradox

As you come to intuitively access awareness of these cosmic dynamics, whether you are familiar with quantum physics or not, inherent paradoxes become increasingly more apparent and seemingly ubiquitous. Recognition, and the ultimate reconciliation of these paradoxes presents a primary quality of activating the eighth circuit. Dualistic perspectives give way to a unitive awareness. What were previously perceived to be opposites become recognized as mere relationships between dynamics. You become able to entertain and process multiple models of reality without conflict—each being accessible to use as interchangeable lenses of observation with which to view the world. You can experience a multitude of mutually dependent, interpenetrating, eminently transcendent realities.

"The void is form, and the form is void."

Universe seems to exist both ever-moving and completely still at the same time. The path to reaching this stage of consciousness may be considered a paradox. Upon searching for it, you reach an inherent conflict: that the search will never be able to obtain its goal. *"If one seeks, he will never find; if one fails to seek he will never find; he must seek without seeking."* There is nothing to find and nowhere to look for it because "it" has been ever-present and within all things at all times. As long as you seek a destination, you will never realize there was nowhere to go the entire time.

These experiences of unitive consciousness often tend to be fleeting. To those who have not experienced it, someone discussing these matters can sound nonsensical, absurd, or even heretical to existing social and cultural systems and norms: "the lips of wisdom are closed except to the ears of understanding." As such, a lot of miscommunication can occur. Yet these experiences have been accessed with enough reliability to warrant discussion as a facet of human awareness/consciousness. This may be the main reason many mystical or spiritual teachings have been kept secret except to those considered qualified initiates.

TRUE COMPASSION

As this circuit becomes accessed more frequently, you may feel filled with an inexhaustible compassion for others as well as with an effortless altruism. All anxieties and fears around death and suffering vanish, allowing you to accelerate your intellect and physical energy without being buffered by psychological hindrances. You may be deeply moved by the suffering of others, but without attachment or partiality; rather, every circumstance is approached on equal grounds. This may appear unemotional to others.

THE DREAMTIME

You can become self-aware during sleep, with increased lucid dreaming. This may be experienced either internally within your body or externally as an out-of-body experience (OBE). Out-of-body, near-death, past-life, and trans-time experiences have all been reported to correlate to the activation of the metaphysiological Circuit 8.

THE CREATOR CIRCUIT

The 8th circuit has been described as the "creator circuit" to convey the increased ability to directly influence reality through interaction with the void and vast expanse of potential. This encompasses the "law of attraction," in which creative power proceeds directly from "source," which is then nourished by thoughts, beliefs and intentions of desired results. A similar process of thought patterns determine form (the course of events can be found in much more technical and mathematical terms in quantum mechanics). Rather than being a passive observer or bound by a fated course, you become an active participant and creator of the structure of the universe.

FINDINGS OF DR. STANISLAV GROF

Following are varying degrees of subjective experiences recorded by Dr. Stanislav Grof relevant to Circuit 8 consciousness.

EXTRAPLANETARY CONSCIOUSNESS

With extraplanetary consciousness, one is said to directly experience phenomena related to celestial bodies outside of our planet, and to astronomical events including conditions on other planets, the sun, supernovas, etc. Related are consciousness experiences of interstellar space, "characterized by feelings of infinity and eternity, tranquility, serenity, purity, and unity of all opposites."

CONSCIOUSNESS OF THE UNIVERSAL MIND

The experience of the universal mind can be described as a sense of being encompassed within the totality of existence and the underlying supreme principles of being: "boundless, unfathomable, and ineffable; it is existence itself." Important components of this experience are said to be intuitive insights into the process of the creation of the phenomenal world. This results in a temporary but enduring feeling of having achieved a global, non-rational, and transrational understanding of the basic ontological and cosmological problems of existence.

SUPRACOSMIC AND METACOSMIC VOID

Grof considered this the most expansive and most paradoxical transpersonal phenomenon. It entails accessing the "primordial emptiness, nothingness, and silence"—this being seen as the "ultimate source and cradle of all existence" and the "uncreated and ineffable Supreme." It is said to be "beyond time and space, beyond form or any experiential differentiation, and beyond polarities such as good and evil, light and darkness, stability and motion, and agony and ecstasy." Causality itself is said to be transcended.

NEUROBIOLOGY

The boundaries between your body and its surroundings that breaks down during Circuit 8 states is associated with the posterior superior parietal lobe. It has been proposed that the broadened sense of connection or oneness, and feelings of unity are likely associated with inhibition of these regions. Transcendent consciousness has shown a harmonization and synchrony of alpha and theta activity with advanced practitioners.

The inferior parietal area may also have associations with mystical experiences. People with lesions of the angular gyrus have reported increased experiences of unity. Neuroscientist Olaf Blanke has targeted the right angular gyrus using brain stimulation, and has been able to produce reports of out-of-body experiences. Selective stimulation of the temporoparietal junction using transcranial magnetic stimulation (TMS) has also elicited experiences described similarly to an out-of-body experience.

A study of non-dual awareness in meditators showed increased functional connectivity patterns between habitually anticorrelated intrinsic and extrinsic information processing neural systems that might correspond to a state of unity of awareness. It has also recently been suggested that one possible construct of non-dual awareness involves the breakdown between endogenous and exogenous stimuli leading to a temporary loss of experiential boundary between Self and the world.

Research has been done in an attempt to account for the neurological foundations of near-death experiences. The following are characteristics of the near-death experience and their proposed neurological correlates:

- Experiencing a "tunnel": Reduced blood flow to the retina of the eyes
- Seeing light at the end of the tunnel: Ambient light and REM visual activation
- Appearing "dead": REM-state paralysis
- Out-of-body experience: Temporoparietal REM deactivation
- Bliss: Reward network activation (dopamine)
- Narrative quality: REM-state dreaming and limbic activation
- Life review: Memory retrieval via hippocampus from sympathetic fight-or-flight activation

It has been proposed that experiences of annihilation—the loss of Self—may be more related to the left parietal lobe, whereas experiences of relational aspects such as connectedness or unity may be more related to the right parietal lobe, although this remains "highly speculative at this point."

CHAPTER LESSONS

- Transpersonal experiences: dissolution of Self where all becomes one, interconnected and inseparable
- Near death experiences/out-of-body experiences with universal expansion
- Waking REM (e.g., the aboriginal dreamtime—walking between worlds where you enter a dreamlike trance while awake) and dreamtime realms
- Quantum entanglement and the implicate order
- Co-creation: intent and thought as a system

GOALS

- Consider/explore implications of universal connectivity
- Explore components and implications of quantum physics
- Consider any periods in your life in which the boundaries of your individual, corporeal Self loosened
- Consider ways that may work to maximize or improve or balance Circuit 8 intelligence in your life

REFLECTIONS

Core Themes: Ego dissolution, non-dual awareness, near-death experience, cosmic consciousness, henosis

Imprint Age: Nonlinear

Mantra: *"I surrender to the unknown." "Into the void I go—to transcend the 'I' and become the whole."*

Describe your understanding of quantum entanglement and the implicate order.

Reflect on the idea that to fully embody who we are, sometimes some part of ourselves must change or die.

Consider the implications of the Self acting as a localized, corporeal interpretation mechanism of a grander, all-encompassing flow of energy and potential.

Imagine and reflect on the concept of multiple simultaneous dimensions and if you were able to travel among them.

Reflect on any near death or out-of-body experiences you may have had. Did you have any significant insight from this experience?

Reflect on the law of attraction and the conscious co-creation of shared experiences.

If you could attract anything into your life, what would it be?

Try to identify people (real or fictional) who embody quintessential C-8 characteristics. What are their strengths and flaws?

____

____

____

____

____

What would the world look like if Circuit 8 were the primary circuit people operated from? What would be needed by you or the universe for this to come about?

____

____

____

____

____

Reflect on the Bill Hicks quote: *"Today a young man on acid realized all matter is merely energy condensed to a slow vibration. That we are all one consciousness experiencing itself subjectively. There is no such thing as death, life is only a dream, and we're the imagination of ourselves... Here's Tom with the weather."* Do you think this statement is a drug-induced delusion or a profound insight into the nature of reality?

____

____

____

____

____

ACTION STEPS

Activities that expand experience beyond the limitations of the physical body. Some examples may include:

- Maintain a dream journal for at least 2 weeks—note any changes in dream frequency and/or quality. Use different colored highlighters to highlight recurring symbolic themes.
- Near-death experiences (NDE)
- Out-of-body experiences (OBE)
- Lucid dreams/REM/dream-state consciousness
- Astral projection
- Visualizing a white or golden light a foot above the head
- Circuit 8 visualizations—white/golden light; dissolution/softening of the Self

IDENTITY RELEASE

Practice "being" without your identity. For an entire day, stop referencing:

- Your name
- Your roles
- Your history
- Your personality
- Your problems
- Your future

Just sit in raw perception. Reflect on what remains when you stop describing and identifying with "yourself."

THE VOID

Imagine approaching the edge of the void—a dark and chaotic infinite space without form. Repeat:

"I can meet the edge calmly."

"The unknown does not require panic."

"I can rest in the vastness of pure existence."

Notice where your system tenses when there's "nothing to hold."

Mini-Ego Death

Practice a mini-ego-death in daily life. For 24 hours let go of:

- Being right
- Being liked
- Being impressive
- Being understood
- Needing to control

Notice what part of you panics. And what part of you feels relieved.

Henosis

Create a simple phrase that inspires feelings of divine union. For example, *"All I am is of the All."*

Say it slowly 3 times.

Notice if your body softens or resists? Where?

End of Life Reflections

If you knew you had 30 days left to live, reflect on what would instantly stop mattering. What would become sacred?

Reincarnation Reflections

List 5 identities you've outgrown throughout your life:

____

____

____

____

Then write: *"I survived every version of me that ended."*

C-8 OUT-OF-BODY EXPERIENCE (OBE)/ASTRAL PROJECTION EXERCISE

Theme: *Non-local awareness, non-physical perception, astral navigation*

Best time: *Late night / early morning (the wake-back-to-bed method is often helpful)*

Goal: *Separation or stable non-physical perception*

This meditation should be studied and memorized loosely to the best of your ability as a guide; you will be unable to read through it and practice it simultaneously. There are astral projection hypnosis meditations available on YouTube and other media sources that may be helpful as well.

Lie down comfortably on your back and gently close your eyes (an eye mask can be helpful, but is optional). Rest your hands on your belly or at your sides. Inwardly affirm, *"I am practicing separation, not sleep,"* and remind yourself, *"My body is safe. I will return."*

Now focus on stabilizing Circuits 0 and 1 to create a foundation of safety and calm.

- Inhale 4 seconds...
- Exhale 6 seconds...
- Repeat for 8 rounds...

Then say internally:

> *"I am so much more than my body. My consciousness is allowed to explore other dimensions and return."*

(Do this every night when you dream.)

Now become the witness... Stop trying to "project," but instead just allow your identity to loosen and shift. Let your body feel heavy, warm, distant. Your job is to remain awake as it drifts.

The next phase is known as the **vibrational phase.** This is extremely common on the pathway to an OBE.

- Bring attention to the center of the skull (the crown, not the forehead).
- Imagine a soft, electric hum building there.
- On each exhale, imagine the hum expanding outward like a field.

It is normal if vibrations arise (buzzing, shaking, ringing, swaying, "engine" sounds, hence the name of the phase). Should you reach this phase, it is imperative to remain calm or you may abruptly end the experience.

- Do not move physically
- Do not analyze
- Do not get excited or afraid
- Just witness the experience neutrally and allow it to happen

There are several **separation techniques.** Choose one method and commit to it for 2–3 minutes:

1. **The Rope:** Imagine an invisible rope above you. Without moving your physical body, imagine "climbing" it with your mind. If done right, your consciousness will pop out of your body.
2. **The Roll-Out:** Imagine rolling to the side out of bed. Don't try hard—just intend the roll.
3. **The Backward Fall:** Imagine you're falling backward into black space. This often triggers instant separation.

Now **stabilize** the astral body. (Many people lose the experience here.) The moment you separate, do this immediately:

- Rub your astral hands together
- Touch a wall
- Look at the floor texture
- Say to yourself: "Stabilize now."

This helps to lock in the environment. Now the fun part: **C-8 Navigation!**

To become more comfortable with your newfound astral senses you can stay nearby and explore the etheric environment just outside your body; or you can go non-local. If you choose the cosmic explorer route, pick ONE target:

Option 1: The Star Ocean: Say, "Take me to the cosmic ocean." Let the scene form.

Option 2: The Oversoul Mirror: "Take me to the place where I remember who I truly am."

Option 3: A Specific Guide: "Take me to the being aligned with my highest good."

Once at your destination, just be present with your experience and allow it to unfold. If anything feels predatory or off in any way, *leave immediately.*

When you're ready to end the experience, say, *"I return to my body gently."* Then wiggle your fingers and feel your physical body. Take a few breaths, open your eyes, and sit up slowly.

Immediately write:

- Sensations
- Visuals
- Location
- Emotional tone
- Any "downloads"

If you had difficulty at any point, here are some troubleshooting tips:

If you fall asleep, use the wake-back-to-bed method:

- Sleep 4–6 hours
- Wake for 10–20 minutes
- Then do the practice

If you get fear in the vibration stage, remind yourself that this is your nervous system changing states. Say, *"I am safe. Continue..."*

If you get stuck in sleep paralysis on your way out, recognize that this is an indicator that you're at the exit point you're seeking. Do not be afraid. Use the roll-out method immediately.

If you see weird entities, treat it like a dream ecology: neutral observation, don't worship, don't panic, and leave if it feels wrong.

Circuit 8 Re-Imprinting Meditation: Death & Liberation

Theme: *Ego dissolution, cosmic unity, remembrance of life's preciousness*

Lie down comfortably and close your eyes. Place your hands on your chest and say inwardly, *"My body is safe. My mind is clear. I can return at any time. I am ready to meet the truth of death."* Allow the body to settle; feel gravity supporting you.

Now prepare for descent...

- Inhale to the count of four...
- Hold for the count of six...
- Exhale to the count 8...
- Repeat three times, letting your body sink deeper with each exhale...

Feel yourself softening, letting go of tension. Imagine each exhale as a gentle release of the story of "you" (roles, worries, identity). Repeat silently, *"I release the need to cling to my identity. When I release the ego, I connect with something greater."*

You now find yourself at the threshold of death awareness. Imagine a doorway at your chest or forehead—a portal into non-local awareness. Step inward with your attention: feel yourself floating beyond the body. Sense the release of life's grip, ego dissolving, identity melting into awareness. Witness sensations: buzzing, warmth, silence; whatever arises, allow it.

Say inwardly:

"It is safe to let go. It is safe to surrender."

As you feel your ego dissolve, your awareness expands into cosmic unity—the most blissful sense of oneness with all of existence as divine consciousness.

- Imagine your consciousness merging with the infinite field of being.

- No edges, no time—just a luminous, knowing presence.
- Feel yourself as both the wave and the ocean simultaneously.
- Silently repeat, *"I am the drop, I am the sea. I am everything, I am nothing."*
- Let love, awareness, and timelessness wash through you.

When you are ready to return:

- Sense a subtle thread reconnecting you to your body.
- Breathe into your chest and belly, grounding.
- Place your hands on yourself again.
- Say inwardly: "I return, carrying the truth of life and death. I live on borrowed time now, free, awake, and aware to live fully my divine purpose."
- Feel gratitude and liberation. Life itself becomes precious, immediate, and vibrant.

Take a moment to integrate this experience...

- Sit up slowly. Observe the body, the room, your senses.
- Note one insight or one intention for how this liberation manifests in daily life and write a daily affirmation reflecting this insight (e.g., *"I am not separate from Pure Being, "Life is a gift borrowed from death," "I carry unity into each moment")*

CIRCUIT 8 INTEGRATION QUESTIONS WEEKLY REFLECTION

- What did I learn about my relationship with death, ego-release, and the infinite this week?
- How has my ability to surrender and return shifted?
- What practices most supported my Circuit 8 activation?
- Where do I still cling, resist, or fear dissolution?
- What does my nervous system need to meet the void with steadiness and peace?
- How is Circuit 8 health affecting my lower circuits and daily life?

Chapter 12

Closing Reflections

As you reach the close of this journey, it is important to see that re-imprinting is not a ladder to ascend away from life, nor a process of leaving your lower circuits behind. True evolution comes not from "ascension" alone, but from integration—bringing the wisdom, clarity, and expansive awareness gained in the higher circuits back into the foundation of your being. In doing so, you raise yourself as a whole to a higher level of intelligence and overall wellbeing—a cycle that can be repeated *ad infinitum*, leveling up your entire existence with each iteration.

The circuits are layers of your psyche and consciousness, each holding lessons, gifts, and patterns to be understood. Through this process, you learn the profound truth that human development and evolution are cyclical, not linear. Each ascent to higher awareness is most meaningful when it feeds back into the lower circuits, repairing early wounds, transforming limiting beliefs, increasing intelligence, and expanding the capacity to live fully.

Re-imprinting is psychospiritual evolution in action—a cyclical process of rising, realizing, and returning. You ascend to witness, to dissolve, and to illuminate; then you descend to repair, integrate, and embody. When integration is complete, each level of your consciousness supports the others, and life itself becomes a laboratory of freedom, wisdom, and love.

Transcendence opens the insights, clarity, and expansive perspective gained in upper circuit consciousness down into the circuits that govern survival, emotional patterns, cognition, and relational templates. By doing so, you can:

- Heal unresolved trauma in the foundational circuits.
- Transform limiting beliefs and self-concepts implanted early in life.
- Integrate ego dissolution and cosmic unity into embodied, practical wisdom.
- Reclaim autonomy and presence in your daily life, grounded in the full spectrum of consciousness.

And so much more!

Finally, remember, the work is never truly finished. And you are not leaving the human experience behind. You are returning to it transformed, carrying the lessons of the cosmos in your mind, heart, and body to live awake, embodied, and conscious of both your ephemeral mortal frame and your immortal awareness. Each day, each encounter, each breath is another opportunity to ascend and return with greater awareness and insight, and to live fully in the harmonized rhythm of all circuits.

Glossary

Anchors: Circuits 1–4 provide stabilizing "anchors" for upper circuit dynamics that may become too chaotic or disorienting

Archetypes (Jungian): A concept from psychology that refers to a universal, inherited idea, pattern of thought, or image that is present in the "collective unconscious" of all human beings

Astral Projection: An experience in which a person's consciousness is said to leave their physical body for a period of time and travel in the "astral plane"

Chapel Perilous: An existential state of limbo, usually full of confusion and disorientation for the ego. A psychological state in which an individual's ego may feel confused, displaced, uncentered, or uncertain whether some course of events was affected by a supernatural force, or was a product of their own imagination. This state may be experienced anytime, though one may be more prone to experiencing it during activation of a transpersonal circuit experience.

Circuit 0: Prenatal and perinatal experiences

Circuit 1: Basic needs, survival, physical security/safety, attachment style (Freud's "oral stage"; Bowlby's "attachment theory")

Circuit 2: Emotional needs, role in the social hierarchy/territorial politics, power dynamics in relationships (submissive versus dominant, autonomy versus dependence; Freud's "anal stage")

Circuit 3: Logic, symbolic thought, language/semantics, writing, mathematics, development of representational mental maps, cognitive processes, executive functions (Piaget's "concrete operational stage")

Circuit 4: Social groups, cultural norms, tribal behaviors, religious/other rites of passage into adulthood, sexuality, morality/superego development, social proscriptions/prescriptions (puberty/adolescence; Piaget's "formal operational stage")

Circuit 5: Pleasure for the sake of itself; ecstatic states (e.g., as attained through yoga, cannabis, ecstatic dance, tantric sex)

Circuit 6: Questioning of one's identity and the influences of conditioning on personality and sense of self; metaprogramming (the conscious and intentional deprogramming and reprogramming of the self in accordance with more internally/transpersonally-defined constructs of personality/psychospiritual identity and individual will (e.g., Crowley's concept of the HGA [Holy Guardian Angel]); conscious and intentional self-transformation and self-actualization

Circuit 7: Astral plane/astral projection; experiences with non-physical/discarnate entities, paranormal/psi experiences, telepathy, the archetypes; psychoid space, synchronicity, inter-generational heredity/genetic memory encoded in one's DNA; accessing past lives, the Akashic records

Circuit 8: Non-dual states, ego dissolution, dream states, near-death experiences (NDE), oneness with the universe or "God"

Co-Regulation: A psychological term describing the continuous and dynamic interaction of two or more individuals who influence each other's emotions and behaviors

Collective Unconscious: A term introduced by psychiatrist Carl Jung to represent a form of the unconscious—the part of the mind containing memories and impulses of which the individual is not aware—common to mankind as a whole and originating in the inherited structure of the nervous system

Critical Periods: Refers to a specific timeframe within which a child "must" acquire certain skills, because if this does not happen, the child cannot easily attain these skills outside this time frame

Cybernetics: The science of communication and control theory that is especially concerned with the comparative study of automatic control systems (such as the nervous system and brain and mechanical-electrical communication systems)

Epigenetics: The science of how environmental influences change the expression of genes

Experiential Metaprogramming Phase (EMP): The acute phase in which an individual undergoes or experiences altered/non-ordinary/transpersonal states of consciousness by a variety of means outlined in this text, or other practices which may induce such a state and allow for a greater ability for conscious metaprogramming, re-imprinting, or self-change.

Hedonic Engineering: Methods of using incoming sensory signals and somatic sensations as a means of experiencing heightened pleasure for pleasure's own sake are discovered and developed

Henosis: A classical Greek word for mystical "oneness", "union", or "unity"

Hermit Phase: A short period of time following the induction or experiencing of a transpersonal or psychedelic state where one is encouraged to reflect on, journal about, and settle back into ordinary consciousness to maximize effective integration or metaprogramming

Holonomic: A system is called "holonomic" if, in a certain sense, one can recover global information from local information. Wherein the whole is contained, to some degree, within the individual part. Derived from "holos" and "nomos", the law of wholeness. Dr. Jenny Wade cites physicist David Bohm's concept of the simultaneous inter-relatedness and interpenetration of all phenomena to her use of the term in her holonomic model of the evolution of consciousness

Holotropic Breathwork: A breathing practice developed by Dr. Stanislav Grof based on his research with psychedelics and non-ordinary states of consciousness to emulate or achieve these states through deeper and accelerated breathing patterns, evocative music, and facilitation of energy release through a specific form of bodywork

Hypoxia: A state in which oxygen is not available in sufficient amounts at the tissue level to maintain adequate homeostasis

Imprinting: The concept that life-events at particular stages of development set patterns that continue to resonate throughout one's lifetime

Imprint Vulnerability: A period or state lending itself to the nervous system or psyche taking on an imprint which it may perpetuate or act as a filter or bias when processing future experiences or states

Inner Healer/Inner Healing Intelligence: The tendency, ability, knowledge, and power within oneself to move towards wholeness and wellbeing

Integration & Reinforcement Phase (IRP): The phase following an altered/non-ordinary/transpersonal state of consciousness and the Hermit Phase in which the individual performs or receives guidance in effectively integrating and reinforcing insights, metaprograms, or re-imprinting

Kundalini: In yogic traditions, the life force that is said to lie coiled at the base of the spine until it is aroused and sent to the head to trigger enlightenment

Lower Circuits (see also: Mundane Circuits): Circuits 1–4 in the original 8-Circuit Model of Consciousness—or Circuits 0–4 in the 8-Circuit Ascension model—relating to personal egoic human development

Lucid Dream: The experience of achieving conscious awareness of dreaming while still asleep

Metamodel: A model of a model or which may encompass multiple models simultaneously

Metaprogramming: Programming or re-programming beliefs, habits, and thought patterns through the action of applied metacognition—thinking about or reflecting on how and why one has certain thought or behavior patterns and the development of the ability to consciously alter these for one's benefit

Morphic Field: Proposed organizing fields of resonance responsible for Morphogenesis of living entities, that memory is inherent in nature, and that most of the so-called laws of nature tend to be more like habits; best known through the works of Dr. Rupert Sheldrake

Morphic Resonance: A proposal by Rupert Sheldrake that morphogenetic fields may be transmitted from past members of the species through a non-local resonance wherein the patterns of activity in self-organizing systems are influenced by similar patterns in the past, giving each species and each kind of self-organizing system a collective memory

Morphogenesis: The origin and development of morphological characteristics

Mundane Circuits (see also: Lower Circuits): Circuits 1–4 in the original 8-Circuit Model of Consciousness (Circuits 0–4 in the 8-Circuit Ascension version) relating to personal egoic human development

Near Death Experience (NDE): An experience wherein one comes very close to dying and has memories of a spiritual experience (such as meeting dead friends and family members, out-of-body experiences, or seeing a white light) during the time when death was near

Non-Duality: A state or experience of unity with all things wherein duality and plurality, and separation of self from all else, becomes experienced as phenomenal illusion. An awareness of matter as materialized energy, and the temporal manifestation of an eternal incorporeal essence constituting the innermost self of all things

Non-Locality: In physics, the concept of action-at-a-distance—that an object's state can be affected by another object without being in physical contact with it; that is, the non-local interaction of objects that are separated in space. In quantum physics, quantum non-locality refers to the phenomenon by which the measurement statistics of a multipartite quantum system do not allow an interpretation with local realism

Parapsychology: A field of study concerned with the investigation of evidence for paranormal psychological phenomena such as telepathy, clairvoyance, and psychokinesis

Pranayama: A Sanskrit word formed by the conjunction of *"prana"* (breath of life/vital energy), and *"ayama"* (expansion/regulation/control). A yogic art of breathing consisting of the deliberate modifications of the breathing process, such as rapid diaphragmatic breathing, slow/deep breathing, alternate nostril breathing, and breath holding/retention, which are usually done in a seated posture

Precognition: Knowledge of a future event, especially when this comes from a direct message to the mind (such as in a dream), rather than by reason

Preprogramming Phase (PP): First phase of metaprogramming. Assessing relevant background information about the journeyer, establishing rapport, assessing the journeyer's prior knowledge about and experience with psychedelics/therapy/coaching and their expectations, addressing safety issues and concerns, providing education, setting intentions, creating a map of the circuits and any imbalances to be worked with, identifying and understanding current reality tunnels and beliefs systems (including mental health history), and setting a plan for metaprogramming. These guidelines can be applied by individuals doing their own circuit work to consider and reflect upon before embarking on their metaprogramming journeys. This approach can be effectively utilized in methods with or without psychedelic drugs

Psi Phenomena: The phenomena (or alleged phenomena) studied in parapsychology, including extrasensory perception, precognition, and psychokinesis

Out-of-Body Experience (OBE): A phenomenon in which a person perceives the world from a location outside their physical body. A form of autoscopy

Re-imprinting: The process of re-coding specific belief structures, memories, or behavioral patterns within your neurology

Shocks: Circuits 5–8 may act as stimulating "shocks" toward development, evolution, or reprogramming within the egoic circuits

Spiritual Emergence: *"The movement of an individual to a more expanded way of being that involves enhanced emotional and psychosomatic health, greater freedom of personal choices, and a sense of deeper connection with other people, nature, and the cosmos"* (Grof & Grof, 1989)

Spiritual Emergency: A form of crisis in which one may experience drastic changes to their meaning system (i.e., their unique purposes, goals, values, attitudes and beliefs, identity, and focus), often as a result of a spontaneous spiritual or transpersonal experience. These may include psychiatric complications related to existential crisis, mystical experience, near-death experiences, kundalini, paranormal experiences, ecstatic states, or other spiritual practices

Synchronicity: The simultaneous occurrence of events which appear significantly related, but have no discernible causal connection. "Meaningful coincidence"

Telekinesis: The production of motion in objects (as by a spiritualistic medium) without contact or other physical means

Telepathy: Communication from one mind to another by extrasensory means

Transpersonal Circuits (see also: Upper Circuits): Circuits 5–8 relating to non-ordinary states of consciousness (NOSC)/transpersonal experiences

Transpersonal Psychology: A branch of psychology focused on studying the spiritual, transcendental, and non-ordinary aspects of human experience

Treadmilling: An instance in which a person becomes rigidly stuck or locked into narrowly operating within a particular circuit

Uncertainty Threshold: How much ambiguity, uncertainty, and change that a person can tolerate; a low uncertainty threshold can result in increased adverse reactions to environmental stimuli (e.g., anxiety, depression, compulsive behaviors)

Upper Circuits (see also: Transpersonal Circuits): Circuits 5–8 relating to non-ordinary states of consciousness (NOSC)/transpersonal experiences

Verticality: Interdynamics and relationship between the personal and transpersonal circuits, wherein the personal circuits may act as "anchors" for transpersonal circuits, while transpersonal circuit experiences may act as "shocks" to imprints or belief structures of personal circuit experience. These relationships are: Circuit 1 anchor with Circuit 5 shock; Circuit 2 anchor with Circuit 6 shock; Circuit 3 anchor with Circuit 7 shock; Circuit 4 anchor with Circuit 8 shock

About the Authors

Dr. Douglas Wingate received his Doctorate in Traditional Chinese Medicine from *Five Branches University,* and his Masters from the *Oregon College of Oriental Medicine*. He has completed postdoctoral studies in clinical neuroscience from the *Carrick Institute,* as well as being a certified Functional Medicine Hyperbaric Clinician, Licensed Acupuncturist, herbalist, and is certified in somatic psychedelic integration. He was part of the first cohort of licensed psilocybin facilitators in his home state of Oregon, and co-owns one of the first licensed psilocybin service centers in the United States. He works with the *Integrative Psychiatry Institute's* psychedelic-assisted therapy program, as well as providing metaprogramming instruction and guidance through *8-Circuit Ascension/The Institute of Applied*

Metaprogramming with co-founder Dr. Rachel Turetzky. He specializes in neurological, emotional, neuro-cognitive, and chronic pain conditions, including working as an adjunct professor at the National University of Natural Medicine, and in the neurology department of *Oregon Health & Science University Hospital.* He has written multiple books on the topics of brain health and consciousness including *Circuits and Shen: Models of the Evolution of Consciousness and Chinese Medicine.* He is a long-time practitioner of meditation, *qigong,* and Daoist internal alchemy *(neidan).* He is also an alumnus of the *Maybe Logic Academy* where he had the honor of studying the Eight-Circuit Model of Consciousness under Robert Anton Wilson.

Dr. Rachel Turetzky holds a Ph.D. in Clinical Psychology with Emphasis in Depth Psychology from Pacifica Graduate Institute. Her dissertation analyzed Rick Strassman, M.D.'s bedside notes from his early 1990s DMT studies. She earned her M.A. in Psychology from The New School, and completed additional research training in a cognitive neuroscience lab at the Icahn School of Medicine at Mount Sinai. She trained in psychedelic-assisted therapy through Sage Institute (now Alchemy Community Therapy Center), and has a certification in ketamine-assisted therapy through Fluence. She has worked with MAPS/Lykos Therapeutics since 2012, predominantly working as an Adherence Rater on their MDMA-assisted therapy clinical trials for PTSD. Dr. Turetzky studied the 8-Circuit Model of Consciousness with Antero Alli in his 8-Circuit Brain course. She is also a Certified Integrative Wellness & Life Coach, Certified Yoga Teacher, Reiki Healer, practices herbalism, and offers holistic lifestyle guidance. She provides psychedelic integration and psychonautic support through Eleusia Psychedelic Integration Coaching, ketamine-assisted therapy through Brighter Life Therapy, PLLC, and offers metaprogramming instruction through *8-Circuit Ascension/The Institute of Applied Metaprogramming* (co-founded with Dr. Douglas Wingate).

For more information, see:

8circuitascension.com

FROM ANTERO ALLI

ANGEL TECH
A Modern Shaman's Guide to Reality Selection

Angel Tech is a comprehensive compendium of insights and techniques for the direct application of Dr. Timothy Leary's Eight-Circuit Brain model for Intelligence Increase. What Dr. Leary posited as theory and Dr. Robert Anton Wilson brilliantly demonstrated in sociopolitical, mathematical and intellectual proofs, Antero Alli has extended into tangible tasks, exercises, rituals and meditations.

THE EIGHT-CIRCUIT BRAIN
Navigational Strategies for the Energetic Body

The Eight-Circuit Brain advances and expands the material presented in *Angel Tech,* a compendium of techniques and practical applications based on Dr. Timothy Leary's 8-Circuit Brain model. After more than twenty years of research and experimentation, Antero's earlier findings are significantly updated and enriched.

FROM ANTERO ALLI

STATE OF EMERGENCE

Experiments in Group Ritual Dynamics

State of Emergence presents a group ritual technology for gaining access to impulses, emotions and sensations through movement, vocalization and action. This somatic work explores a dynamic visceral interpretation of Jung's 'active imagination' for making the Unconscious, conscious that can enrich any ritual, dance and theatre practice as well as anyone ready to start their own creative ritual group for self-discovery.

EXPERIENTIAL ASTROLOGY

From the Map to the Territory

Experiential Astrology revisions the horoscope as a map to access the autonomous forces represented by the planetary symbols and the twelve archetypes of the zodiac. By changing the traditional terms of 'planets, houses and signs' to 'Forces, States and Styles', the author invites you on a journey to discover the very heart of the human condition. Features interpretive techniques culled from over thirty years of astrological study and practice.

FROM ANTERO ALLI

THE AKASHIC RECORD PLAYER

A Non-Stop Geomantic Conspiracy

The Akashic Record Player is based on a true story, inspired by the author's unexpected 7th circuit activation (ref: Leary's 8-Circuit Brain model), and his attempt to integrate these mystical experiences with the help of people he met on his journey back from "the center of the earth." It's a story about miraculous interactions, sifted through a mythic, allegorical context. Myth is the very language of life, and through its articulation, we become more alive.

THE BIG BLACK BOOK

Become Who You Are

With Christopher S. Hyatt, Ph.D. and friends

Most sections of *The Big Black Book* were written by Christopher S. Hyatt along with his friends and colleagues between 2003 and 2008, and were originally published as individual booklets. Now the entire series has been collected into this single volume. But what is *The Big Black Book* about? Little more can be said lest we give away its intent and reduce its impact.

FROM ANTERO ALLI

A MODERN SHAMAN'S GUIDE TO A PREGNANT UNIVERSE

With Christopher S. Hyatt, Ph.D.

The Pregnant Universe is a Neural Cocktail party of a brain getting drunk on itself. It is the essence of slimy copulation between known and unknown forces. As the planet braces for a series of new contractions, bizarre and interesting forces are being born—brains with new centers, new chemicals, new visions—going far beyond the suited dinosaurs prattling their slogans.

REBELS & DEVILS

The Psychology of Liberation

Contributions by Antero Ali, Wm. S. Burroughs, Timothy Leary, Robert Anton Wilson, Aleister Crowley, A.O. Spare, Jack Parsons, Genesis P-Orridge, and many, many others.

"When he put the gun to my head at 16 I left home…" So begins this remarkable book which brings together some of the most talented, controversial and rebellious people *ever.* Not to be missed!

FROM ANTERO ALLI

PARATHEATRE

A Ritual Technology for Self-Initiation

Since 1977, Antero Alli has been developing a ritual technology for Self-Initiation—Paratheatre—combining techniques of theatre, dance and zazen to access and express the internal landscape. Paratheatre is highly transformative, and has served as a critical source of inspiration for many of Antero's artistic endeavors, especially his films. (Audio)

8-CIRCUITS OF CONSCIOUSNESS

In this video, Antero Alli discusses his research results and a wide variety of perceptions on Timothy Leary's 8-Circuit Brain model for Intelligence Increase. Antero introduces the origin of this system, and how his interpretations differ from Dr. Leary's and Robert Anton Wilson's, along with his insights on the vertical connectivities between upper and lower circuits, the function and nature of shock, the first and second attentions, and much, much more.

FROM ANTERO ALLI

TO DREAM OF FALLING UPWARDS

The elder Magus just passed away. Jack Mason, a promising young sex magickian cultivated to advance the lineage, loses it all when the elder Magus' biological son unexpectedly inherits everything with plans to commercialize and franchise the Temple. Jack plots deadly revenge and falls into a dizzying maze of encounters with underworld characters, desert brujas, and a twist of fate he never saw coming…or did he? (DVD)

UNDER A SHIPWRECKED MOON

The power of a long-dead family secret is unleashed when the rituals of a self-made shamanic punk rocker catapult him into the spirit realm in search of his father, a ship's captain who drowned at sea. Meanwhile, back in the real world, he and his family gather around the bedside of his grandfather who has suddenly reappeared after a fifteen-year absence. A surrealistic fable of love, giant hedgehogs, and the mystical depths of family bonds. (DVD)

www.ingramcontent.com/pod-product-compliance
Lightning Source LLC
LaVergne TN
LVHW052321200926
848481LV00002B/627